Praise

'I'm glad *Angry Mother Assertive Mother* exists. Cristalle shows us mums how to befriend, accept and channel our anger in a healthy way. Filled with useful journal prompts and exercises, *Angry Mother Assertive Mother* is a worthwhile read for any mum feeling ashamed of their anger and keen for change.'
— **Miranda Fairhall**, psychotherapist and founder of Attune For Connection

'If you are a mother trying to make sense of your feelings of anger and frustration, then *Angry Mother Assertive Mother* is the book for you. It offers an insight into the experience of many mothers today, combining psychological understanding with helpful, practical suggestions. Even though the topic is quite challenging, Cristalle Hayes' writing style makes it an easy and compelling read. I will recommend the book to my clients.'
— **Miriam Chachamu**, family, couple and individual psychotherapist

'Why is it so hard for a mother to say she is angry? What is it within us, within society that makes this so taboo? *Angry Mother Assertive Mother* lifts the lid on this maternal pressure cooker to explore what's really going on and suggests ways of navigating these explosive (and very normal) feelings. For the angry voice inside us all, this is a welcome addition to the shelf of typical parenting books.'
— **Dr Charlotte Hatton**, Chartered Educational Psychologist, HCPC Registered

ANGRY MOTHER

Assertive Mother

From maternal anger to radical repair

Cristalle Hayes

R^ethink

First published in Great Britain in 2021
by Rethink Press (www.rethinkpress.com)

Cover image © Shutterstock | Valenty

Sysiphus illustration by Judith Wardle, all other illustrations by Laura Vahabzadeh.

This book is not a substitute for therapy but may be beneficial when read alongside working with a therapist. If you are triggered by anything covered in this book, please reach out to a therapist for help to process and work through any issues that resonate with you.

To the lovely one and my brilliant boys

Contents

Foreword

When Cristalle asked me to contribute to her book on angry mothers, I was intrigued. I could immediately identify my own maternal anger, but also experienced a surprisingly strong sense of shame and guilt. I was grateful and frightened in equal measure at being invited to explore this. As I read the book, I was astounded at the common themes of shame and guilt and the heaviness and destructiveness of suffering in silence. I was also relieved and comforted to see how much sense my own anger made within the context offered in the book.

Being a mother in this lifetime is different to being a mother in past generations. While there are enduring similarities, there are also huge differences. There seems to be more isolation, pressure, criticism and unfairness. There is also an increasing recognition and understanding of the impact of trauma on birth and motherhood.

Anger is often defined as a strong feeling of hostility or aggression and commonly associated with behaviours that cause fear or discomfort. It's widely seen as a negative emotion, and certainly one that females are encouraged to reject as unfeminine and undesirable. But anger can also be a useful and positive emotion. Intimately, it is a warning; a normal human response to being under threat from physical or psychological harm. When we consider the common feelings of powerlessness, unfairness, humiliation, shame, guilt and sadness, as well as being disrespected and criticised, it becomes clear why maternal rage exists.

When we use suppression to routinely manage our anger, it diminishes our self-awareness and has a detrimental effect. Suppressed anger doesn't just go away. Repressed and ignored anger is now recognised as a factor in many women's illnesses. In my work with mums, they frequently share their shame, lack of support, lack of self-belief and guilt. There is pressure to work, to stay at home, to breastfeed and to bottle-feed. There is stigma and judgement at every turn. I frequently see how this contributes to poor maternal mental health and, sadly, the impact of this on future generations. With children and young people, I often hear about the impact of parental anger. I also commonly see that these young people have not developed a healthy relationship with their own anger and ways of expressing it.

Books on anger are frequently focused on how to 'manage' this emotion. Indeed, books on parenting are full of advice on how to be a 'better' parent and foster deeper attachment. This often results in more shame for those mothers who experience rage rather than the gentle, loving connection we want to achieve. Anger can be a powerful drive for change. It can often act as a force, or momentum, to incite change. In writing this book, Cristalle has created a profound and necessary call to action for our society to understand, acknowledge and support the experience of mothers today.

The book aims to address some of the causes of maternal anger, exploring social and cultural factors, as well as the impact of trauma and of current expectations of motherhood. It offers a non-judgemental explanation of the unfeasible position many mothers find themselves in, as well as some really useful strategies and activities to help mothers recognise and process their own feelings and needs. As such, the book is enormously helpful for mothers, fathers, students of psychology and counselling and mental health practitioners. It's a fresh perspective on maternal anger which is both bravely honest and refreshingly supportive of women undertaking the enormous challenge of modern motherhood.

Emma Taylor
Counsellor and associate lecturer in counselling and psychotherapy, University of Central Lancashire
www.positivestepscounselling.co.uk

Introduction

I never wanted to be an angry mother. I never wanted to feel rage around my children. I had spent my life afraid of anger and trying not to be an angry person. For me, angry people were those who had lost control and were potentially dangerous. I hadn't realised that anger and rage were different. All I knew was that anger was unsafe, and I didn't want to be an unsafe mother. I was shocked to discover that motherhood rendered me angry, frustrated and impatient: all the qualities that I felt were the opposite of being a good mother. This side of myself bursting out blindsided me. Uncomfortable and nauseous, I raged when pregnant. I fumed in John Lewis when a woman told me not to bother buying a bottle because breastfeeding is much better for a baby. Why can't she mind her own business, I thought to myself.

I was frustrated when a healthcare professional didn't take my fears about the neonatal intensive care unit (NICU) seriously. I was shocked and hurt when my first baby was born via emergency C-section and the midwife called me a spoilt child who didn't like pain. I raged when I saw my baby in the NICU surrounded by sick babies. I raged at the powerlessness I felt at being unable to take him home with me, that I couldn't breast-feed him and that I couldn't settle him while he was attached to the tubes. I rolled my eyes when the next-door neighbour expressed concern about who would look after my baby when I went back to work. 'Oh, I'll let him fend for himself; he is, after all, nine months old now.'

I raged when I was woken up from a deep sleep by a crying baby once again. I raged at people who were sleeping more than me. I raged at obnoxious noises from cartoons and plastic toys. The constant interruptions, the perpetual laundry, my toddler who wouldn't sleep, my husband who did sleep, the constant mess, my colleagues progressing in their careers while I remained stagnant. I raged at all of this. I kept all this burning rage inside and tried hard to be the calm, nurturing, loving presence that a mother ought to be. The mother I *wanted* to be. Why was I feeling so much rage? What was I doing wrong? Why wasn't I enjoying this?

Motherhood was more complex than I had realised. I loved being a mother. I remember staring at my sleeping baby in the middle of the night and grinning until my cheeks hurt. I felt so proud of my baby. I was excited to walk around the park with him in a pram. I proudly took him to the local library and to the playground. I delighted in his ability to go down a slide and take his first steps. I listened to all the nursery rhymes and learnt all the actions and words to the songs. I wound the bobbin up, I hopped little bunny hop-hop-hop and I zoomed-zoomed-zoomed. I listened to all the advice and tried to take it on board, even though much of it was conflicting and different to what my own mother was advising.

I discovered that the older generation were told different things to what mothers are told today. I learnt the delicate balance of listening to outdated advice without offending the advice-giver who was only trying to help. I blended purees and researched toys and milestones. I chatted to new mum friends and we shared our struggles and comedy moments over coffee and banana cake. I eagerly waited for the next chapter in my child's life. I loved my child and our relationship. I was so proud of him and loved him for simply existing.

However, this joyful energy was mixed with a darker, angrier energy. My emotions felt constantly heightened. I experienced everything in high definition. Intense joy, but extreme anxiety, fear and anger. Why did nobody warn me about this? Why wasn't this mentioned or taken seriously by healthcare professionals? I appreciated that our bodies go through immense changes when we become mothers and hormonal shifts change how we experience our emotions, but it felt more profound than hormones. It felt more than sleep deprivation. The anger felt like it was coming from a place deep inside of me. Suddenly, I was invisible; I didn't matter. My freedom and my choices were not being respected. My self and identity were disappearing.

When my second baby was born, the rage intensified and was harder to contain. Then the Covid-19 pandemic happened and we were all thrown into lockdown. The pandemic took all my usual methods of self-care away and left me feeling unsupported. I was too overwhelmed to find new ways to stay calm and grounded. I started drowning, and I became angrier and angrier. I refused to make space for my anger because I did not want to be an angry mother. Being a therapist, I knew the value of therapy and would have loved weekly sessions with a compassionate therapist, but when did I have the time? The internal battle was intense. Even with all my skills and tools as a therapist, I couldn't resolve this anger on my own.

One sleepless night, my overtired second baby wouldn't stop crying. He wouldn't feed and he wouldn't sleep. I was exhausted. I was alone in the night. I felt powerless to calm him and myself enough to feed him and help him sleep. The internal rage felt so strong and my thoughts became dark. My body felt tense and my jaw ached with the effort of grinding my teeth. I was so far away from where I wanted to be as a mother. That's when I knew I needed to get a handle on maternal anger. I needed help; I couldn't do this on my own. I needed a new plan and a different perspective. I needed to create a roadmap to navigate anger around my children. I needed to make space for my anger and to take it seriously.

I started talking to other mothers about maternal anger and realised that I wasn't alone. Maternal anger was something that resonated with many women. What struck me was how much mothers struggle with maternal anger and rage while navigating the profound and complex experience of motherhood. The more I spoke to mothers, the more I understood. Mothers are angry not only because parenting can be stressful and hard, but also because they need more support, freedom, respect, equality and self-care. Mothers are feeling invisible, powerless, disappointed and overwhelmed.

Maternal anger and rage are there, but they remain in the shadows of motherhood. The problem is that if anger remains in the shadows, unspoken and unreflected, it can become more violent, more toxic and more abusive. It can turn into rage. Motherhood then becomes a stressful, unhappy and potentially damaging experience. What mothers need to know is that motherhood may well provoke anger. Anger in itself isn't a bad thing. Anger is a healthy human emotion that we are entitled to feel. It is what we do with the anger that counts: how we listen to it, take responsibility for it and understand it. Your anger is not you, but energy within you. If we are going to express anger around our children, we need to figure out how to do so safely.

After speaking to mothers, I understood that mothers want to understand their anger and reduce their angry outbursts around their children, but feel ill-equipped. *Angry Mother Assertive Mother* doesn't tell mums to 'calm down and carry on', but provides a clear roadmap to help mothers navigate their maternal anger and rage. It equips mothers with the confidence, tools and language to make space for and reframe their anger, to connect with and communicate their anger, and to repair after the rage. It's about making positive changes with our anger.

The first part of *Angry Mother Assertive Mother* is about how we can think about anger, maternal rage and motherhood. What is anger and where does it come from? I will shine a light on the different themes and experiences which provoke maternal rage. Journal prompts throughout the chapters will help you explore your anger, and exercises in listening to your body, mind and inner child through guided meditation and guided bodywork are provided. We will also explore how we can harness the power of our anger and use the power of maternal anger to make positive changes.

The second part of *Angry Mother Assertive Mother* is about communication and repair. I will explore how mothers can communicate their anger directly and respectfully to their partners and their children. The essential part of maternal anger is how we repair after rupture. I will discuss repairing with compassion and trauma-informed self-care.

I have included stories and quotes from mothers I spoke to at length on their experience of maternal anger and rage. I have anonymised these anecdotes by changing details and names and often combining more than one story. My intention was to create an overall sense of what mothers are experiencing, as if we were all sitting and talking honestly about our anger over coffee and banana bread – something which, I believe, doesn't happen nearly often enough.

While I attempted to speak to as many mothers as I could, I am aware that there are many voices and experiences that I have not listened to and may not be represented in this book. We live in a world which has (consciously or unconsciously) a bias towards white, middle-class, heterosexual, married parents. This bias is often apparent in mainstream parenting books but I have attempted to challenge it throughout the book and hope that the mothers who feel invisible and less mainstream will feel their voices are reflected here too.

Angry Mother Assertive Mother will help mothers to:

1. Appreciate what is going on for them when they are angry

2. Make space for anger

3. Feel able to withstand their anger and rage

4. Harness the power of anger and express it clearly and safely

5. Be more in control of anger

6. Unpick and understand triggers to anger

7. Communicate anger confidently to partners and support system

8. Repair after anger ruptures

9. Model a compassionate and respectful way to be with anger around their family

10. Develop a toolbox of meaningful grounding and self-care practices

I wrote this book as a mother of two beautiful boys and as a woman who has struggled to find her voice in her anger. I wrote this book as an existential and trauma-informed psychotherapist who has shared therapeutic spaces with women navigating their anger. I wrote this book weaving in the many voices of mothers from different backgrounds, ethnicities and circumstances to gain further insight into the experience of maternal rage. I appreciate the struggle women have with anger. It is a struggle that is both universal as well as unique to each individual woman.

I am still an angry mother, but I am OK with this. I have found space around my anger. I have learnt how to take responsibility for my anger without beating myself up for it and shaming myself for having strong feelings. My anger is now more of a decision and a choice rather than a reaction. My anger has become less mean and toxic. Anger is a healthy emotion that signals when something is wrong. It is a necessary emotion that doesn't have to be dangerous and unsafe. I have more choice and freedom around anger. The more I understand why I am angry, the more I can have a say in being angry. The more I voice my anger, the more the rage quietens. I am still an angry mother, but I am also a happy mother, a calm mother and a mother obsessed with my children. There is room for everything.

I hope the stories, exercises, journal prompts and my experience help you to quieten the rage, express your anger with assertiveness and repair with compassion and self-care.

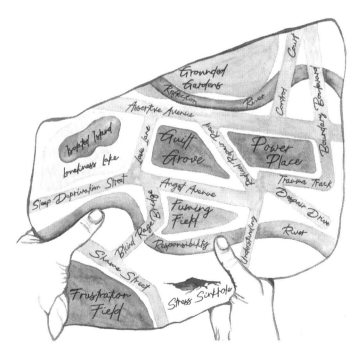

The roadmap for navigating maternal anger

ONE

An Exploration Of Anger

Every mother I spoke to has a story to tell about how anger manifests in their daily lives as parents. While each of these experiences was unique, there was also a lot of common ground. What became clear is how complex anger is. Anger is an emotion that is not black and white and can be thought of on a spectrum. It has many different colours, sounds and shapes and it swings from one extreme to another. Anger can be constructive and destructive. Anger can serve us and be a valuable part of our experience of motherhood or it can be toxic and harmful. It can be both at the same time.

To understand maternal anger, I want to explore what anger is, what role it serves, and your relationship to anger. How does anger manifest in your life as a mother? How does your context of motherhood impact your experience of maternal anger? What value does anger bring to your experience of motherhood? Let's begin our journey navigating maternal anger by first understanding what anger is for you.

What anger is for you

What do you imagine when you think of the word anger? Do you imagine something destructive and violent? Feminine or masculine? Strong or weak? Dynamic or stuck? Painful or vibrant? Anger is a universal emotion that we all experience; a secondary emotion to other, more painful and complex feelings such as fear and hurt. Anger (along with emotions such as joy, sadness, disgust and fear), is neither intrinsically good nor bad. What makes an emotion negative or positive is how it is understood, harnessed and expressed. Anger has a bad reputation, but it can be a profoundly valuable aspect of our lives as women and mothers.

When was the last time you were angry? What was going on just before you felt anger? Anger shows up when we need to pay attention. Anger alerts us when we are under a perceived attack, when something feels unsafe, when we are not getting our needs met or when we feel our values are under attack. We can think of anger as our protection. It protects us from harm and keeps our identities and sense of self safe. Anger can bolster us to stand up for ourselves when we feel we are unfairly treated. Anger tells us when we need to change a situation. The call to change is what I like: anger creates change and motivates us to disrupt the status quo. Anger fights back against injustice.

Anger shows up when we are hurt and gives us the strength, the energy and the power to assert ourselves and make necessary changes. Anger shows up when we are experiencing challenging situations. Motherhood is challenging, so anger may well show up here. It does so in many different ways. Internal, external, slow and heavy or quick and energetic. Anger may be a heavy, suffocating feeling behind our depression and sadness or it may show up in our anxiety. Anger shows up when we are in a rage – shouting and being violent, toxic and destructive. *Rage is anger being disrespectful.* Sometimes we need rage to push back against hurt and abuse, but being on the receiving end of rage can be damaging, confusing and painful – even traumatic.

Children should never be on the receiving end of rage. If rage is the only way you can express your anger right now, please try your best not to express this around your children. I know you do not intend to be destructive or toxic, but there is potential for harm.

Please don't feel judged or ashamed if this is where you are right now – I appreciate how we can get to a place of anger being expressed as rage. I hope to help guide you through a process where you can learn to make space for your anger and to develop strategies so the anger shows up as you being assertive rather than toxic.

How to be angry

One of the key differences between healthy anger and toxic rage is reflection and responsibility. If we take responsibility for our emotions and what is happening to us and around us, anger can be a positive and healthy part of motherhood. Accountability is also crucial when it comes to anger. Without accountability and responsibility, we lose respect and care for ourselves and others. To foster accountability and responsibility, we must learn to lean into anger, tune into it and seek to listen and understand. This process is what I am inviting you to do so that your maternal anger is more likely to be expressed in a healthy, valuable and constructive way.

Passive anger: This is anger that remains hidden, internal, kept within your inner world. When passive with anger, you are not showing the world that you are angry; you may not even disclose your anger to yourself. For some people, this feels the safest way to be with anger. When you are passive with anger, those around you will be unaware of the anger you are carrying. The potential of anger is to create change, so the danger of suppressing anger is that changes won't come about if anger isn't being expressed. Within the context of maternal anger, an example of passive anger would be a mother who has become so fearful or ashamed of her anger that she never discloses it to herself or others when she is angry.

Different types of anger

A mother's fear of anger might be understandable if she grew up in a home where there was a lot of shouting and arguing (too much anger made her feel unsafe) or if she grew up in a home where being angry meant attracting attention to herself, being shamed or being misunderstood. These experiences can feel like highly valid reasons to be passive with anger. Being passive with anger as a child may have kept this mother safe, but it may not work for her as an adult and a mother.

Being passive with anger means that there is a risk of agreeing with everyone to keep the peace, but she isn't keeping the peace with herself. For instance, if her mother-in-law says something that upsets her, she doesn't show it to keep the peace, so the upset remains within her. This passiveness undermines how this mother truly feels about the hurtful comments of her mother-in-law. She is betraying herself and, at the same time, her mother-in-law may be unaware of the impact her hurtful comments are having and so does not have the opportunity to change her behaviour and make amends. When the anger leaks out (as it eventually will), it can leak out indirectly. This is how we get to passive-aggressive anger.

Passive-aggressive anger is an indirect expression of anger. It is anger that doesn't appear to be anger. Going back to the mother who feels hurt and criticised by her mother-in-law, she may not feel it's appropriate for her true, angry feelings to be revealed. She wants to express how she feels but wants to avoid the potential confrontation and messiness that may result if the anger is expressed. The mother will express her anger in other ways, for instance, she may stop inviting her mother-in-law over. She may turn up late to her mother-in-law's house or 'forget' to buy her a birthday card. The mother may withhold information about her daughter's school play. She may slam cupboard doors or roll her eyes whenever her mother-in-law comments on her daughter's behaviour.

The risk here is that the mother is still not giving either herself or her mother-in-law the opportunity for honesty and repair. The critical comments may be the mother-in-law's anger coming out. Neither side knows why the other is angry. This dance can be exhausting and hollow, and can further deteriorate relationships and inner peace. Eventually the build up of unexpressed and unheard anger may get too much and when the mother-in-law makes a comment that hurts the mother, her response will come out as aggression.

Aggressive anger has a force to it and is expressed in a destructive way such as rage, violent outbursts, humiliating comments, insults and swearing. A person may express their anger with aggression if the anger is overwhelming and too much to contain. Aggressive anger feels powerful, but the hurt and vulnerability underneath the anger is not being expressed or seen by the other person. The mother-in-law on the receiving end of aggressive anger or rage will feel attacked and confused by this response. The mother is airing her anger, but there is much potential for misunderstanding and further hurt.

Assertive anger is when anger is expressed directly, creatively and respectfully. When anger is reflected upon, understood and validated, anger becomes an outward expression and falls within the relationship between the angry person and others. The anger is a part of the conversation and a part of the relationship. This anger is dynamic and does not feel as painful and fraught as the previous types of anger. The message underneath the anger is expressed and heard.

Assertive anger feels cathartic. To express her anger to her mother-in-law in an assertive way, the anger could be phrased like this: 'I find it undermining when you make comments about my parenting. I need to trust my own decisions. Is there a way you can support me in my choices around parenting?' This statement isn't accusing or attacking her mother-in-law, but clearly expressing how she feels, and why.

An assertive statement is about you and not the other person. Setting a rule in place can help. Even if the other person continues to make hurtful comments, at least you know you have set down rules so everyone in the situation is aware of what you will and won't find acceptable in communication.

Ultimately, I have found it easier, more effective and less painful for myself and others when I express my anger in an assertive way. Clearly and directly, I understand my intention behind the anger and the message my anger needs to convey. This ability is hard-won, and isn't easy and always possible. Even when we express our anger in an assertive way, it doesn't mean that we can fix the issue at hand. We also need the other person to be able to reflect and be assertive, clear and direct. I will explore more on communication further on.

The complex relationship with anger

To appreciate how it can be difficult for some women to be angry in a powerful way, we need to start unpicking a woman's complex relationship to anger. A woman's relationship with anger is informed by how they experienced anger growing up. Young girls are not encouraged to be as angry as boys and men. Anger is often associated with masculinity and power. Women are meant to be softer and passive. Women often feel they need to navigate their anger on their own and internalise it. One of the women I interviewed expressed how she has often felt that her anger wouldn't be taken seriously as a woman.

Mary's story

As a child, whenever anyone became angry around me, my response was to make myself small and bland. I didn't want to attract attention, fuel the flames or

23

make the situation any worse. I desperately wanted the situation to change and go back to being calm again. I found anger confusing and scary. When I was angry growing up, people responded by immediately calming me down and soothing me. This reaction annoyed me as it made me feel that I couldn't just be angry, that my anger was wrong somehow. Whenever I got upset or frustrated, my parents would react as if I was crazy, out of order, acting up. I would find this attitude confusing because they were allowed to be as angry, but I couldn't be. When I am angry, I am bewildered as to whether it is OK to be angry. It just feels too much.

Women don't always feel as powerful as men and may need to express their anger with words rather than with physical strength. Women may doubt their anger, often wondering if they are overreacting, or if anger is expressed, that they will appear weak and not taken seriously. Women often minimise their anger internally. How often have you felt angry and then when someone asks, 'What's the matter?' you lie by replying:

- 'Oh, it's nothing. I'll get over it.'
- 'I'm probably overreacting.'
- 'If I tell him I'm angry, it'll only cause an argument and he won't change anyway.'
- 'What's the point? It won't change anything.'

Women often feel that being angry won't make any difference to the situation. I can hear the powerlessness in these statements. Even if you feel powerless to make changes (which isn't necessarily true), you need to honour yourself and your values by voicing your anger.

Journal Prompt

Take some time to reflect on and explore your experience of anger growing up. How did people express their anger around you? How did people respond to your anger?

Different cultures also have a vastly different relationship to how anger is expressed. Some cultures embrace the passionate expression of frustration and anger. Other cultures have a 'stiff upper lip, keep calm and carry on' philosophy around anger. Different cultures will also have different levels of tolerance for women being angry. Why do we feel we need to calm women down? Women also relate differently to anger depending on their generation. Historically, angry women have been called terms like nag, shrew, hysterical and mad. Having this in our history as women means we carry a sense of shame around anger. We may need permission to be angry and may only feel comfortable being angry around other women. We may be suppressive or passive-aggressive with our anger as this feels like the only safe way we can be angry without being judged or shamed. Even as I wrote this book on maternal anger, I found myself asking for permission to write it: was this OK? Would I get into trouble for shining a light on a complex and hidden topic?

Bringing maternal anger into the light

Maternal anger is a complex, taboo and confrontational subject to discuss. Mothers don't want to be perceived or judged as angry or in a rage. Many of the mothers that I spoke to want to appear in control, happy and enjoying motherhood. Not just appear to be, but to actually be ports of calm and nurture, loving and protective figures. What happens when a mother does get frustrated and angry? What happens when motherhood taps into our shadow side where rage lurks? What happens if this anger isn't brought into the light? The danger is that unreflected anger can become dangerous and harmful.

Maternal anger takes many forms. Maternal anger may take the form of shouting and swearing, throwing something, pushing, hitting, or emotional, sexual or physical abuse. Maternal anger can also look like constant or occasional humiliation with unkind words or dirty looks – an inability to see the child's perspective and only see their own. Maternal anger can also look like withholding kindness and care. Anger can look like neglect. Anger can look like a silent treatment. When a mother is angry, they may handle their child a little bit too roughly, throwing their baby into the cot or grabbing their toddler's arm with too much strength so it hurts them. Maternal anger can look like shouting at your toddler for behaving like a toddler and not like an adult. Maternal anger may not be directed at the child but expressed on social media or to friends and family members (hurtful if the child ever sees or hears this). All these expressions of maternal rage can be painful and harmful to your child. Physical assault and abuse against your child is illegal. If you recognise yourself in this behaviour, I hope this book can help you move towards maternal anger, which is expressed directly but with safety, care and respect.

If you feel your anger is becoming harmful, please reach out for further support from a therapist or health worker. I have also included a list of resources at the back of the book.

Maternal anger doesn't have to be, and isn't always, destructive and harmful. Mothers can express maternal anger in an assertive and contained way. The message behind anger can be communicated with intention and purpose – a will to protect and parent and not harm. Parents can harness maternal anger so the relationship between mother and child isn't ruptured, but there is needed change: a change in values, levels of safety or behaviour. Maternal anger can look like a mother shouting at a child running across the street without looking. The mother may be so afraid for her child that she may have yelled and yelled, even though the child was safe from harm. Maternal anger can look like a mother pulling their child off a sibling during a fight. The mother

uses her physical power to break up a fight before anyone gets hurt. Motherhood can present us with some
extremely challenging and stressful situations where
we have to think and react on the spot. It might not be
until later that a mother may reflect and think of other
ways to have handled the situation. Sometimes mothers already have the wisdom, but not the emotional
space, to react as they would prefer.

There are many different expressions of maternal anger being expressed in homes. Women are not being
praised or recognised for the times when they have
managed to express their anger safely and with respect. Women are being judged and condemned when
their anger has turned to rage. While this is not OK,
not enough energy and care is being spent understanding what gets mothers to this place of uncontrollable,
violent anger. Tools are not given to mothers on navigating their maternal rage, so they often feel powerless. Mothers left in a place of powerlessness over their
anger often feel intense guilt and shame. This only
leaves them more vulnerable to rage and less likely to
reach out for support. That is why it is so important to
bring anger out of the shadows and have realistic conversations about maternal anger. Mothers can support
each other, and health professionals can support mothers through their anger without the guilt and shame.

The issue is that motherhood doesn't always give wom-
en the time to process strong emotions and intensely
tricky situations. There often isn't space to pause and

take a breath and reflect on what is going on externally and internally. Motherhood can often feel like relentless provocations when we are sleep deprived, stressed, hungry and overwhelmed. Much of what happens is a reaction and mothers may feel quicker to anger than before they became mothers. Despite their best intentions, mothers are still human and vulnerable to falling into a rage in a challenging situation.

We need to listen to what is being said behind the rage. Maternal anger can mean many things, but it doesn't necessarily mean that you are a bad mother or have bad children. It can mean a mother has reached her limit and her anger is her way of fighting back. At the same time, children are doing what they are hardwired to do and push our boundaries when we don't need them being pushed. It is possible to stop the anger from spilling out into rage. While at times it seems impossible, it is possible to find space to stop, reflect and process. Finding and claiming that space is essential for mothers to reduce angry outbursts and to control how they react.

Kathleen, a mum of three children (sixteen-year-old twin girls and an eleven-year-old boy), spoke candidly about her challenging experience of maternal anger. Being a qualified counsellor and now in her forties, she has a new understanding of her rage. Kathleen had her first child at the age of twenty-three, an adult, yet close enough to her angry teenage years. Her maternal anger at the time came out as unreflected rage. She described it as feeling like she wasn't even in her own body. One moment she would be fine, and then suddenly, almost like an out-of-body experience, she'd be in a rage. With hindsight she realises that at the time, she was being catapulted back into a powerless child state. Rage was the only way she could express herself and let people know that '*I exist here. I am important in this situation*'. The rage would come out as a scream. She'd be known to stand in front of her fourteen-year-old child, screaming and screaming. Kathleen said it usually happened after she had already asked, and asked, her middle child to stop fighting with his brother and sister. There are only so many times when you can say, calmly, 'please stop fighting'. Her most rageful moments were when she felt she had to think of the needs of all her children and needed to protect everyone in the room.

Kathleen's experience shows how maternal anger can manifest, yet at the same time, how it can take a lot of pressure and urgency to push a mother to reach this place of rage.

While at times it seems impossible, there are ways to find space to stop, reflect and process. Sharing experiences between mothers can be an invaluable way of finding and claiming this space to contain angry outbursts and to control how they react, as told by this mum:

'When I was pregnant with my first children, a dear friend gave me invaluable advice. She said, "There will be moments when you will want to throw your baby out of the window. Please don't be alarmed by that. Obviously, don't do it. You will feel it though. Recognise it just as a feeling; it will pass." I am very grateful for that advice. Nobody tells you how parenting can bring you to the edge of sanity. Nobody warns you.'

Who is motherhood?

The myriad of mothers and their contexts adds another layer of complexity to maternal anger and rage. Motherhood comes in many different shapes and sizes. We may all be sailing in the sea of motherhood, but we are all sailing different boats. Some may have a motor and some may have oars. Some boats may have many different people inside and some mothers may just be sailing along with their children. The family makeup influences the experience of motherhood and anger setup. There are single mothers, working mothers, part-time working mothers, and stay-at-home mothers. Much of the advice given to me when I had a newborn baby suited a married, stay-at-home mum, but I often thought to myself, 'What about mothers who don't have a partner? What about mothers who have full-time work?'

Single mothers have a unique set of challenges that mothers with partners don't have. Many of the single mothers I spoke to said that they often feel that they have to be the mother and the father all in one. They find it tough to take on both roles and switch from more masculine energy to feminine energy. Single mothers spoke about how they don't have another parent to bounce ideas and situations off. They have to figure out the parenting road independently. I listened to single mothers and felt grateful and privileged to have a partner to let off steam and have someone to talk it through with if I don't think something went well. If it is a safe and healthy relationship then having a partner is one way to diffuse anger. Without that, where does the anger go? A single mum of twins discusses her challenge:

> 'Their dad doesn't have anything to do with
> their lives. He doesn't see them at all. Doesn't
> talk to them on the phone. So, it's tougher. I try
> to be mum and dad in one. I alternate. I have
> to be super-strict like dad and then be more
> like myself. I have to be both parents because I
> don't have that other person. I can't call in that
> other person and say, "You bloody deal with
> this one."'

Mothers raising neurodiverse children in a world and society that is more set up for neurotypical children have a different set of challenges. Mothers of children with dyslexia, dyspraxia, ADHD and ASD expressed anger towards a public who judge their children and an education system that seems unfair for children who struggle academically. Mothers watch their child struggle to master to ride a bike or learn to read or make friends while their friend's children learn these skills and have these experiences in a way that appears effortless. Mothers with neurodiverse children will have an extra fight on their hands to get a diagnosis, a team of therapists to help, and get the education system to help with their child's needs. Mothers are raising children with a whole range of disabilities. There are also mothers with chronic illnesses and disabilities themselves. All of this presents a unique set of challenges and mothers may experience anger that these challenges are taken for granted. When I was seventeen, I was given a formal diagnosis of dyspraxia, now known as Developmental Coordination Disorder (DCD). This condition affects balance, spatial awareness, coordination, short-term memory and information processing. It means that sometimes, especially when I am very tired, my body and mind won't allow me to do the most basic activities (such as following simple directions, fiddling with straps on a buggy or cooking without breaking or spilling things). I find being dyspraxic extremely frustrating at times, and this only adds to my anger and frustration. Learning to have a bit of acceptance and compassion around my limitations has helped. I have a lot of empathy towards mothers who are also battling with conditions such as dyspraxia, ASD, ADHD and dyslexia.[1]

---

1   https://dyspraxiafoundation.org.uk

Speaking to lesbian-identifying mothers co-parenting with their female partners, there was a layer of anger over the hurdle of even becoming a mother. Many lesbians don't have the privilege of falling pregnant quickly. Money, time, anxious waiting and invasive fertility treatment may eventually lead to a baby, or it may not. Women in a same-sex partnership create a family in a society generally biased towards the traditional family setup with a mother, a father and three healthy children. A lesbian, bisexual and transgender experience of motherhood will differ from parent to parent and family to family and there can be anger and frustration at the bias, judgements and difficulties unique to these mothers.

The narrative and advice surrounding motherhood doesn't always consider that many mothers are also in employment. Many of the mothers I spoke to felt under enormous pressure from the expectation to work as if they don't have children, and to mother as if they don't work. The average mother in the UK has a job[2] and can't be a full-time mother to their child, but much of the parenting still falls on their shoulders. For some mothers, their job is a great way to let off steam and have a break from being a parent, but it is more complex than that. The associated guilt can

---

2   ONS, 'Families and the labour market, UK: 2019
     (Office for National Statistics, 24 October 2019),
     www.ons.gov.uk/employmentandlabourmarket/
     peopleinwork/employmentandemployeetypes/articles/
     familiesandthelabourmarketengland/2019, accessed 9 September
     2021

feel overwhelming at times – guilt for not performing well at work and guilt for not performing well at home.

Motherhood is also made up of women who have complex dynamics with their own mothers. While some mothers have a close relationship with their own mums, those who have a complex or no relationship with their mothers can feel isolated and unheard. Seeing other mothers with close relationships can be a painful reminder of what they are missing. Mothers are also bringing up children while grieving the loss of their mothers. Grief while parenting adds more pain, which can show up as anger.

Unfortunately, the scope of this book means it isn't possible to include every context of motherhood but hopefully this overview has shown how complex this is. The good news is that we can make changes once we recognise and then unpick and unravel the layers and complexities of our situations.

Journal Prompt

- Create a sketch or artwork of your 'anger monster' representing what anger means to you.
- How does your situation and context as a mother impact your maternal anger?
- How does maternal anger show up in your day-to-day life as a mother?
- How comfortable are you with expressing anger?

- How do people around you respond when you express anger?
- How do you experience maternal anger? Is your anger constructive or destructive?

Summary

This chapter has explored anger as an emotion and its different forms and roles in your life. It has explored how a woman's relationship to, and experience of, anger can influence her maternal anger. It has also looked at what maternal anger is, and the ways it can manifest. Lastly, it has reframed motherhood to create a different perspective on anger, as mothers will have a unique experience of motherhood depending on their context.

TWO

Maternal Burnout

Mothers are angry because of the mental load of motherhood. The thinking, planning and responsibilities that fall on a mother's shoulders create a constant feeling of having all these things to do, not enough time to do them, and the fear that it will all fall apart if they don't get done. Mothers are angry at the lack of a 'village', a feeling that they are doing this alone. Parenting decisions and values feel undermined by society and in-laws.

Mothers are angry as they suffer the inequality between gender roles. Mothers are angry because of a lack of support and respect – two things they most certainly deserve. Mothers are angry because they don't have enough space for self-care, which leads to self-neglect. Mothers are angry because their children won't stop fighting. Mothers are angry because their child had another tantrum and refused to eat another home-cooked meal. Mothers are angry because their child is being bullied. Mothers are angry because their teenager is not doing their homework or their teenager is taking drugs. Mothers are angry because they see how society treats different people differently and their child is different from the mainstream.

There are so *many* reasons why mothers are angry. All these thoughts, feelings and experiences are burning angry holes into mothers. Some are valid at face value, and some may take more unpicking and unravelling to get to the root of the anger. In this chapter we'll explore these reasons, which can be summarised as maternal burnout.

Maternal burnout is the feeling of being burnt out. Our flame is extinguished by the many different tasks, anxieties, worries and stresses that motherhood piles onto us. Many are unseen and unexpressed. Many are obvious. Research by a team at The Gottman Institute led to an understanding that anger is often a mask or cover for deeper emotions and they were the first to coin the term 'anger iceberg'.[3] Above the surface is anger, but underneath the surface there are many more vulnerable feelings hidden, such as sadness, loneliness, insecurity and fear. While we

---

3   S Regan, 'How to use the anger iceberg to work through conflict & emotions' (mbgmindfulness, 28 June 2020), www.mindbodygreen. com/articles/the-anger-iceberg-and-how-to-work-with-it-effectively, accessed 19 August 2021

Maternal anger iceberg. Adapted from research by
The Gottman Institute, www.gottman.com

carry all these feelings around we can easily become
burnt out, and that will manifest as anger. When we
are burnt out, we don't have the internal resources to
handle the stress of motherhood. Mothers are burning out because of the mental load of overwhelming
responsibilities.

The mental load is there partly because of the inequality between mothers and fathers and the different expectations and perceived roles of men and women. Women inside a family setup find themselves in a position where there is an overwhelming amount to do. They naturally take on board most of the responsibility and have to navigate careers and other life responsibilities at the same time. Mothers are more likely to burn out even further when there is no village to support them. Self-care is essential to prevent maternal burnout, but there is often a lack of time and self-care opportunities. Mothers lack a village and cannot prioritise being their own village. There is often an internal struggle to put their own needs first. No wonder mothers are experiencing so much maternal anger.

Where is my village?

'It takes a village to raise a child' is an African proverb and is actually an embodiment of many different African cultures and their attitudes toward parenting. I support this sentiment, and there were many moments during the Covid-19 pandemic where I felt the lack of a village. 'Where is my village?' was also a familiar cry from the mothers I interviewed. 'I just can't do this on my own.' Doing everything alone certainly felt more intense with the lockdowns and social distancing that the pandemic created. The lack of a support network, or 'village', lay underneath maternal anger.

Motherhood can be a profoundly rewarding experience, yet the day-to-day experience of motherhood can often feel relentless, exhausting, repetitive, stressful and demanding. Motherhood demands time, patience and energy. It demands mothers to be constantly interruptible. They can often find themselves pushed to their limits. Many mothers feel a sense of unfairness in this. 'Where is my village? Where is my support when things get so tough that I need backup?' Hardworking mothers recognise that there needs to be someone to take over when they're exhausted and pushed to their limits. Many of the mothers I spoke with said they often felt alone and unsupported.

The pandemic left many mothers with a lack of basic, essential support. Lockdowns, social distancing and overwhelmed NHS services meant that mothers were supported even less than usual. Baby groups and breastfeeding support groups weren't running face-to-face and children's centres and soft plays were closed. This left mothers feeling more isolated and less supported. A new mother now has to work extra hard to get support. Even when the effects of the pandemic pass, these experiences will stay with them. Where is the space to process these experiences so it doesn't feed into their maternal anger?

Your experience of what you found supportive will be different to another mother. For instance, some mothers have had a positive birth experience and felt that their midwives and healthcare professionals were supportive.

Suzy's story

With my first child, I found many of the midwives I came across to be unsupportive and shaming. One midwife accused me of being a 'spoilt child who didn't like pain'. The lack of respect and kindness made me angry, but I didn't feel I could say anything. I felt that I shouldn't complain and I that I couldn't reach out for help. I needed to internalise my suffering. I feel angry now when I think of other mothers who may have a similar experience. The experience I had with my second baby at a different hospital was different. I found all the midwives and nurses incredibly supportive, respectful and caring. The difference in support made a profound difference in my mood and confidence as a mother.

Not all mothers are able to find a support network. If you don't find it easy to connect with new people, then you will find these situations harder. Seeing other mothers quickly making connections can compound loneliness and feelings of inadequacy. Not having a supportive group in a similar position to rant over WhatsApp or a coffee when it all gets fraught and stressful can lead to mothers further internalising their feelings of anger. Some mothers found their National Childbirth Trust (NCT) group to be an absolute lifeline, while other mothers found it to be isolating and lonely, as they didn't connect with those mothers. Many mothers are unable to access an NCT group.

Some mothers feel incredibly supported by their partner at times, and at other times not at all. No person can give us 100% support all the time. Some partners shine in certain areas of support and don't in other areas and that can be hard, especially when we compare ourselves to how much support we perceive our friends to be getting. Some mothers are unsupported because they don't have partners. They may be divorced or not with their partner, or their partner may be abroad, work long hours, have a chronic illness or be emotionally unavailable.

Mothers may also lack support from their own mothers. There are motherless mothers out there, mothers who don't have a good relationship with their mother, and mothers who can't ask for support from their own mothers because their relationships are too complicated or they are estranged. Motherhood can highlight the lack of support from those around you, especially when you see mothers with their partners helping out in playgrounds and mothers with their mothers. Scenes like this can make mothers angry, especially on days when their children are being particularly challenging or after a sleepless night. Julia, mother of a two-year-old girl, says:

'What I found hard after giving birth was the lack of support. That freaked me out. I am an immigrant here. I don't have any family here, and we were on our own. It was a difficult birth. It was shocking; I was traumatised. It made me so angry, and it made me feel like shit that nobody cared about me.'

Sleep deprivation is a massive issue for mothers. Unless you have lived it, it can be complicated to convey how hard it is to function, let alone be accommodating, patient and available to your family. A mother of a boy and a girl says:

'I often felt frustrated, as "tired" was not a good description of how I felt. The exhaustion was so profound, and I wished there was a particular word for existing on so little sleep. I became obsessed with not sleeping more than four hours in a row. My son was five before this became a reality (my son had an undiagnosed condition). I felt like I was on another planet, and it deeply affected my relationships and my health. I napped when I could. When I look back, I wish I had found some way to get help.'

The importance of self-care

Self-care is essential to survive the stress of motherhood and should be actively encouraged by the village or support system that surrounds mothers. Through integrating self-care, mothers will naturally feel calmer, less burnt out and less quick to anger. A mother is responsible for their child's basic needs: safety, hygiene, nutrition, mental health, happiness, education and developmental. They ensure that their children sleep well, eat well, play well, share well and generally develop into decent human beings. Motherhood comes with a vast amount of responsibility in the quest to raise the next generation. They need to take care of themselves and put themselves first to do this properly. Self-care should be actively encouraged and accessible for a mother and seen as a priority by her support system. When this isn't the case, mothers will remain angry.

When mothers do not actively make self-care a priority, they neglect their needs in a way that they would never neglect the needs of their children. Of course, it's hard to give yourself the same care you give your child, but the concern is that society currently celebrates the mother who feeds herself last. We're in danger of seeing sleep deprivation as a badge of honour. The mother who can only relax and take care of herself once the children are asleep is seen as both normal and acceptable. What if we replaced the word care with respect? What if we say that mothers are not giving themselves the same respect they give their families? Why is it so difficult for society to accept that mothers are deserving of care and respect? Society needs to give mothers the recognition they deserve and recognise how much mothers are giving and not receiving. I remember when I took my eight-week-old baby to see the health visitor. She said to me, 'I always made sure I ate first.' That stuck with me.

There is a focus on self-care for mothers in the last chapter. I have called it 'radical' self-care as it may seem a radical idea for mothers to put their self-care needs first. Let's all encourage each other to put ourselves first; this is a great act of self-care.

Equality and the mental load

The list of invisible, often intangible, tasks involved in running a household and being a parent creates a mental load. It is a constant cycle of planning and organising domestic life, and it is often the women who take this mental load on board. During the pandemic, many women noticed how easy it was to find themselves in the role of the cliched 'fifties housewife'. Mothers can feel that they aren't treated as equal to their male counterparts, but find it hard to break out of the gender roles.

I noticed this when people commented that my husband was such a 'hands-on dad'. No one was complimenting me as being a hands-on mum. People assumed I would take on the responsibility and role of motherhood with grace and ease, and that it didn't need recognition. It seems that the hard work a man puts into parenting is far more easily recognised and celebrated. This assumed responsibility is certainly making many mothers angry, but in the generations before us, fathers weren't generally involved in day-to-day parenting. Women that I interviewed often commented that people would ask them, 'Is your husband babysitting tonight?' He isn't babysitting. He's a parent. (To be fair, attitudes are gradually shifting and I think that this question is also annoying to dads.)

The gender-specific roles and outdated attitudes still ingrained in society have an impact on mums. It's hard for women to break out of their roles. Julie says:

> 'You feel constricted by having to be the primary person responsible for the whole domestic sphere. It's a role that creeps up on you. While working hard at school, it didn't occur to you that what would count when you were thirty-eight would be keeping the house clean. You never realised that is what life was going to be.'

The women of today are breaking the mould, but there isn't anyone modelling for us. Women may look to their mothers for advice, guidance and support, but they may not get this because of the role their mothers played. Sometimes, women may not be aware of the societal setup until they become mothers and see how their male friends and colleagues progress through life unhindered by having children. For instance, I assumed that the male public toilets would have changing tables, but many don't. What do men do when they are with their baby and need to change a nappy? Is it just assumed that the dads are all at work and won't be the ones changing the nappies?

This will gradually change as the current generation of mothers try to redefine the mould. Much has changed since my mother had young children. Expectations are changing. Dads are attending births. Dads are stepping up more to do night shifts and nappy changes. They are shifting their working week around so they can help share the responsibility of parenting. There is still a struggle for women to be treated as equals, though. While this struggle is making mothers angry, it can also be an opportunity for women to harness their anger, forge their way through this and make changes. This need and motivation for change came out in the conversations I had with mothers. C, mother of a sixteen-year-old girl, says:

> 'When I look back on my time as a new mother, there was a strong feeling of, "I've had enough of this. I need more space to think." There was an underlying resentment bubbling just below the surface; an unmet need underneath the anger. At the time, I wasn't clear with exactly what it was at first. I wasn't at peace with having that need. There was a need for having a life that resembled a bit more like I had pre-child, but I knew it wasn't possible. I could see that men, by and large, were less impacted by parenthood. They were less affected by sleepless

nights; they could still watch the rugby, have a job and go to the pub in the evenings.

'I was surrounded by men keeping the job, the hobby and the social aspect. I think a lot of anger was, "What is this? Here I am, preparing bottles, sterilising things and changing nappies." There was a lot of accepting my role and unaccepting my role. There was a lot of unreflected rage. I couldn't say, "I don't like this," let alone ask for my needs to be met. It felt like I was pissed off in general with the world. Now my daughter is a teenager, I recognise why I'm angry, and if it's because I'm not getting what I need as a woman, I can figure out how to get what I need. I learnt to accept and embrace and value my role as a mother, making me a lot less angry. I also learnt to set aside time for myself, and that made me a lot less angry.'

Every household is unique but these are just a few examples of the types of things that create a mental load:

- Food planning, shopping, preparation and cooking
- Organising toys and clothes
- School run, school admin and homework
- Nutrition, hydration and exercise
- Planning outings, activities and playdates
- Appointments and medication

Power of freedom and choices

'What do you mean sleep when the baby is sleeping? I want to sleep *now*.' I would get so frustrated at people telling me, 'Sleep when the baby is sleeping.' I was exhausted and I needed to sleep but instead I had to put energy I didn't have into getting a baby fed, comfortable and asleep before I could rest. The unfairness of this situation would make me so angry. One day I overheard a mother saying, 'I sometimes feel like I'm in prison.' This sentence resonated with me. It made me realise that it wasn't just me in this situation. Many of the mothers I spoke to described feeling powerless and trapped, which often led to resentment and anger. A mum of a six-year-old boy says:

> 'There are a lot of things when you are
> a mother that get framed as choices, yet
> whatever choice the mother makes feels like
> a crappy compromise of finances, time, work
> pressure, family dynamics and what can end
> up at the bottom of the pile is the mental health
> of the mother. You may assume that you are
> the one in charge, and you may think that you
> have agency, and that battle for the agency will
> leave you feeling angry and frustrated.'

Mothers that I spoke to described feeling trapped physically and emotionally: feeling trapped by the mountain of laundry, feeling trapped by a crying baby and a wilful toddler who won't play ball, or feeling trapped at home unable to pursue their careers. Mothers can feel mentally trapped with anxieties and obsessive and compulsive thinking. Mothers can feel physically trapped on the sofa underneath their baby breastfeeding and cluster feeding. Mothers may also be living in a situation where they feel trapped by an unhappy, or even abusive, partnership.

Sisyphus

It is hard to see any freedom you still have and easy to feel frustrated with a lack of freedom. Often, when I find myself consumed with the everyday tasks of being a mother, running a household and running my private practice, I can resent the time spent doing more mundane tasks such as washing up. It can feel that each day is like the Greek myth of Sisyphus pushing a boulder to the top of the hill only to have it roll back down to the bottom overnight and then having to do it all over again in the morning.[4] It is easy to lose sight that while we may feel trapped in this position and have limited freedom and choices, there is a greater context behind it all. We are not just the lady washing up dirty dishes and an object of nourishment for our baby. Mothers are raising the next generation. My husband often reminds me that my children greatly appreciate all the hard work, even if they don't express that appreciation. This reminder expands my sense of power and freedom.

How much freedom, power and choice we have is also about perception. If we perceive we are in prison, that is going to make us angry. We are going to wake up angry and go to sleep angry. Every time we notice that pile of laundry or our child spills their food on the floor or won't go to sleep, we will get angrier and angrier as it is a perpetual reminder of our lack of freedom, power and choices. One mother I spoke to said that when she feels powerless as a mother, she finds herself tidying up, getting a bit too involved in her children's lives and getting frustrated when they mess the room up or misplay the game or don't colour inside the lines. These actions are about her need to feel powerful and in control.

---

4   A Camus, *The Myth of Sisyphus* (Penguin Books, 1975)

My personal experience

Do you ever feel 'touched out' as a mum? Sometimes the touch of our child can feel wonderful, but it can also feel claustrophobic and too much, and this is OK. I feel this lack of freedom and choice when I have spent a long time getting two small children to sleep. My children love cuddles and kisses, and I choose to rock them to sleep. Once they are asleep, I want to be left alone physically. I have noticed I will get angry with my husband for wanting a cuddle or a foot-rub as soon as I come downstairs. This anger is unfair. He wants to reach out and connect and be intimate with me, but in that moment (and for a good half an hour), I need to reclaim my freedom and choices by asking for space and time to myself. Then I can reconnect and be intimate with my husband.

What can intensify maternal anger and rage is when our freedom and choices as a mother are disrespected. As soon as I gave birth to my first baby, I was shocked to discover that my choices around parenting and feeding weren't entirely respected. I often felt challenged by my decisions. I would then be left feeling unsure about my choices. Respecting the choices mothers make empowers them to discover the best choices for their families. A mother of a two-year-old girl says:

'In the hospital, I was desperate to go home. I stayed in the hospital for three nights. They constantly checked on me, but it was like I was living in some film where they did whatever they wanted to me. I felt I had no choice. I chose to breastfeed and needed support. They did try with breastfeeding, and it didn't work. Nobody could figure out why, so I felt like I was some alien who wasn't even able to do the most basic thing which women are created for. Nobody would refer me to someone else. I felt that people didn't care about my choices; the attitude was, "We tried, but it didn't work, so what's the point?" It made me so angry, because I was like, "What the hell? This is what I want!"'

Mothers need to feel that they have freedom and choice because there are so many things that they don't feel in control of. Many of the mothers I spoke to felt that their NCT classes hadn't prepared them for the reality of motherhood. They had been given the illusion that they would be in control, especially during the birthing process. Mothers I spoke to generally entered the birth process with a plan of what they wanted; a sense that they had a choice over what would happen. Having that choice taken away (even if it is the medically correct thing to do in certain situations) made many mothers angry. Necessary medical intervention can be complex because mums that go home with a healthy baby may feel that they can't be angry. New mums need permission, support and the space to process all of this. Mary says:

> 'Lack of control is a huge issue. You are no longer the main protagonist in your life decisions. There isn't much you can do about it. You can't cast it away, as things will disintegrate. It will all be your fault, and you will suffer major criticism for failing. You are kind of in a bind.'

If you are a mother who has undergone trauma, then having your freedom and choices taken away as a mother and woman in labour is even more devastating. The following chapter looks at mothers who have undergone traumatic, painful and adverse life experiences.

Journal Prompt

- When do you feel your most accessible, supported and respected as a mother?
- Who are you with, what are you doing, and where are you?
- When do you feel most controlled, unsupported and disrespected as a mother?
- Who are you with, what are you doing, and where are you?

Summary

This chapter looks at how maternal burnout due to lack of support and the mental load of motherhood contributes to maternal anger and rage. It also looks at how mothers feel an issue with inequality within male and female partnerships and an imbalance of expectations around the mother's role and the father's role. Addressing this imbalance adds to the maternal load and creates further burnout. Mothers feel that motherhood impacts their identity, their freedom and their ability to make choices. At the same time, the medical profession and the network around new mothers may communicate in ways that dismiss a mother's choices and autonomy. Mothers may feel less angry if they have more support from a 'village', partners and society as a whole as well as greater freedom of choice.

THREE

A Painful Journey Into Motherhood

Ideally, we will all arrive at motherhood without having experienced too much pain, stress and trauma, but realistically, life can throw us many challenges and adverse life experiences. The impact of these can be more profound than we realise. Painful and traumatic experiences can impact our trust in others, ourselves and our environment. They can affect our ability to maintain healthy boundaries and regulate our emotions. The impact of trauma can cause us to be mistrusting, fearful, hypervigilant, spaced-out and easily overwhelmed. Simple triggers can throw us back into the grips of a trauma state. What happens, then, when we become a parent?

The impact of trauma

Pregnancy connected me to my body in ways I wasn't expecting. I became attuned to all bodily changes, sensations and emotions. I became much more sensitive to the outside world. My skin felt paper-thin, and I was highly protective of the growing seed inside me. I remember the world seemed to shift from a place of safety to a place of risk. I felt I was constantly standing at the edge of a cliff. The sense of danger made me so angry. I was furious. I shouted at a woman who was riding her bicycle on the pavement and got too close. I felt frustration at anyone who smoked around me. Constantly assessing risk made me uptight, edgy, super-alert and snappy. Ordinarily, I would be far more easy-going and chilled out. I was also feeling guilty about how all this anger may be impacting my unborn baby.

I went for a pregnancy massage in the hopes that it would help me, but it didn't. I felt even worse, and during the massage, I started to internally rage. Every touch on my body made the anger build, until I finally had to stop the massage and walk away. I cried for an hour in a nearby park. What was going on? I hadn't felt this way in a long time, not since I was a child. It suddenly occurred to me that I had felt like this as a child after a traumatic experience. I had felt angry, super-alert and jumpy and hated being touched back then, and this was how I was feeling now. Fear and grief were underneath the anger running through my pregnant body and mind.

I was in a trauma state. My pregnancy had triggered bodily memories. The feelings surrounding unprocessed and painful events were emerging as if they were still happening. It was as if my body didn't quite realise that, in the present, I was safe. The anger thought it was protecting me and keeping me safe, but I didn't need it. I *was* safe. I needed my brain and nervous system to understand that the memories it was experiencing were past pain from past experiences. I shared this with my therapist and realised that I needed to process my childhood trauma and adverse childhood events. I found eye movement desensitisation reprocessing (EMDR) therapy enormously helpful in doing this.

EMDR is a powerful therapy developed by Francine Shapiro in the nineties after a chance discovery. It facilitates the mind's natural process of healing from traumatic events using eye movements or tapping. As Shapiro was walking one day, she noticed that her left to right eye movements seemed to be making her thoughts less distressing. The mind and body are incredible. Most of the time, your body routinely manages new information and experiences without you being aware of them. However, when something out of the ordinary happens and you are traumatised by an overwhelming event such as a car accident or being repeatedly subjected to distress such as childhood neglect, your natural coping mechanism can become overloaded. This overloading can result in disturbing experiences remaining frozen in your brain or being 'unprocessed'.

These unprocessed memories and feelings are stored in the limbic system of your brain in a 'raw' emotional form rather than in a verbal 'story' mode. This limbic system maintains traumatic memories in an isolated memory network associated with emotions and physical sensations; disconnected from the brain's cortex, where we use language to store memories. The limbic system's traumatic memories can be continually triggered when you experience events similar to past painful experiences. Often the memory itself is long forgotten, but the painful feelings such as anxiety, panic, anger or despair are continually triggered in the present. Your ability to live in the present and learn from new experiences can become inhibited. EMDR helps create the connections between your brain's memory networks.[5]

I have attempted to infuse the tools of EMDR throughout the chapters focusing on trauma and maternal anger. It is important to recognise self-care that is trauma-informed – many self-care practices that are encouraged may not be appropriate and create more distress and destabilisation. For instance, having a massage may be profoundly calming and relaxing for some people, but for others it can be retriggering and frightening, especially when pregnant and more vulnerable to touch.

Trauma is not black and white. It is helpful to think of trauma on a sliding scale. In her article discussing

---

5   F Shapiro, *Eye Movement Desensitization and Reprocessing (EMDR) Therapy: Basic principles, protocols and procedures* (Guildford Press, 2018)

various types of traumas, Elyssa Barbash describes the 'big T traumas' such as near-death experiences, car accidents, sexual assault, exposure to war and terrorism, abuse and traumatic loss. Then there are 'small t' traumas – the minor, perhaps less apparent, traumas such as a painful breakup, feeling belittled and humiliated by a parent or partner, redundancy, divorce and chronic work stress. Trauma can also be a single event or more complex, such as domestic abuse, childhood abuse and neglect, chronic work stress or living with an addiction.[6] It is helpful to consider the different traumas you have carried with you to motherhood. All these traumas can be profoundly impactful. The mental health organisation MIND is one of many that confirms that stress signals can continue long after the trauma is over, affecting how you think, feel and behave.[7]

People who have suffered trauma will experience a lot of anger. When the brain and nervous system are reminded of our past trauma, we naturally respond for the sake of self-preservation. There are four responses to trauma:

1. Fight: Fighting, struggling, protesting

2. Flight: Hiding or running away

---

6   E Barbash, 'Different types of trauma: small "t" versus large "T"', Psychology Today (13 March 2017), www.psychologytoday.com/gb/blog/trauma-and-hope/201703/different-types-trauma-small-t-versus-large-t, accessed 20 August 2021

7   MIND, 'Trauma' (MIND, January 2020), www.mind.org.uk/information-support/types-of-mental-health-problems/trauma/effects-of-trauma, accessed 27 August 2021

3. Freeze: Feeling paralysed or unable to move

4. Fawn: Trying to please people around you to protect yourself from being harmed

These are innate physiological and psychological responses that we have no control over – a bit like being tickled. Fight mode can look a lot like anger, frustration, shouting, agitation and restlessness. Our body and mind become mobilised and aroused as we wait to attack the symbolic tiger that our brain thinks is going to eat us. Underneath this is fear. This experience is intense and often out of our control until we learn how to recognise what can trigger us and process the triggers. The reality of going into fight mode because of trauma can seem frightening and confusing when we are with our children. I was in fight mode when pregnant, and until I fully appreciated what was happening, the experience was confusing and upsetting.

An environment of safety and love is essential for the healthy growth and development of children. A nurturing family environment, sadly, is not always the case. Trauma can begin in childhood. The shocking statistic is that one in four girls and one in six boys will be sexually abused before turning eighteen.[8] Childhood traumas such as sexual abuse, physical and emotional abuse have a devastating impact. Childhood trauma will impact how you experience preg-

---

8 Statistics from UK charity One in Four, https://oneinfour.org.uk, accessed 30 August 2021

nancy, birth and early motherhood. It's a complicated reality that the experience of motherhood may bring you close to your childhood trauma, however much you have worked through and healed from these traumas. Having children can provoke strong, powerful, painful and complex feelings, including (and perhaps especially) anger.

This is what often gets missed in the narrative around maternal anger and motherhood in general. The vulnerability to anger from being exposed to trauma is not something expectant mothers are warned about or supported in.

When it comes to trauma, there should only be acknowledgement, but your anger may want to blame, attack and seek revenge. You may feel this type of anger strongly when you are with the vulnerability of your baby, and if you are not aware of this unconscious process, you may feel shame and guilt for responses you can't control.

For mothers struggling with childhood trauma: please remember that whatever trauma you experienced as a child should not have happened. It is not your fault. I am happy you are here and have survived through the pain.

Survivor parents need extra support because trauma adds a painful layer to an already challenging experience of being a mother. Motherhood is challenging for all women. If you are a woman who has survived childhood adversity, the experience is more intense and overwhelming as you also have to navigate your triggers and trauma responses. Sadly, there is still a stigma around childhood trauma, making it harder for new mothers who are survivors to access support. This stigma needs to be broken, which is why it is so important to talk about childhood trauma. Trauma often remains hidden due to shame, but there is healing in speaking our truths. Sharing stories and bringing light and air to our hidden secrets is the best way to eliminate shame. The more we can talk about childhood trauma and its impact on motherhood, the more we can get rid of the shame.

There are many other painful experiences we can carry with us from childhood into adulthood and motherhood:

- We may have witnessed domestic violence as a child.

- We may have grown up around uncontained arguing, shouting and conflict.

- We may have grown up in a home where there was a high dependence on alcohol or drugs.

- Our parents may have been emotionally absent.

- We may have witnessed our parents' divorce.

- Our parents may have gone into hospital or abroad, creating a separation.

- We may have suffered illnesses and invasive medical procedures.

- We may have had to care for our siblings or parents.

- We may have grown up around the stress of financial hardship.

- We may have experienced racism and discrimination.

- We may have been bullied at school or had a difficult, lonely time at boarding school.

These are all experiences that leave anyone feeling emotionally and physically unsafe. Experiences that left you confused, feeling neglected or unloved will create trauma memories. Hopefully, there's been repair and the trauma has less of a profound impact on you now. If more repair is needed, motherhood can be a profound opportunity for this to happen.

Challenges facing survivors of trauma

Living through negative, painful and stressful experiences creates many challenges for mothers. During pregnancy, there are many medical examinations, including internal examinations and scans. These physical sensations may make some women feel uncomfortable or trigger an intense feeling of fear and anger. Unwanted physical touch can provoke a fight, flight or freeze response in us. The physical touch of breastfeeding can provoke feelings of anger and disgust. Even the physical touch of your child may trigger feelings of anger, especially if you already feel like you need some personal space and the touch is unexpected. All the physical, hormonal and emotional changes in your body can make you feel out of control within your body, which may feel extremely painful and unsettling if that has been a traumatic experience in the past.

If you experienced a bad, abusive, traumatic or stressful childhood (for whatever reason unique to you), the feelings and thoughts from your childhood may emerge when you have children. You may feel an extremely strong need to protect your children because you know the real dangers that exist. The thought of them being in danger or at risk may feel so overwhelming that it stops you from taking them out of the house, allowing them to do activities or allowing others to look after them. Survivors of childhood trauma can feel highly anxious about their children being abused, or even that they may abuse their children.

Once these feelings get too much, we can easily disconnect and dissociate. We may space out when alone with our children and feel guilty that we are not as present with our children as we need to be. Confusion and shame born out of trauma responses may be at the root of maternal anger and rage. More support and information for survivor parents would make motherhood a much less lonely and frightening place to be. If you can relate to any of the ten examples of the impact of trauma on survivors below, your behaviour may be trauma related:

1. Anxiety over not wanting other people to look after your child.

2. Burning out as you take on all the responsibility of parenting to keep your child 'safe'.

3. Feeling anxious when others hold or play with your child.

4. Feeling anxious when people around you or your child express anger.

5. Being startled at unexpected noise or movement.

6. Feeling that you need to co-sleep with your child or something terrible will happen to them.

7. Needing to control all situations around your child.

8. Eating too much or too little to mask or control your body and feelings.

9. Feeling vulnerable to shame. (This manifests as feeling criticised when someone offers advice.)

10. Intrusive thoughts and compulsive behaviours.

Additionally, unhealed and unprocessed trauma can lead to behaviours and conditions in adulthood that may worsen with motherhood. These include:

- Depression / anxiety / panic attacks

- Chronic shame / low self-esteem

- Learnt helplessness

- Eating disorders / self-harm

- Addiction

These challenges are understandable, considering what you have gone through. They are based on fear and the need to control. Underneath it all is a sense that you weren't protected or made safe as a child, so you want to keep your own children safe. Looking at anger in this context may give you compassion toward your anger.

My experience with trauma and anger started in pregnancy. It was also highlighted by the experience of having both my babies needing to spend a week in the NICU. While their lives weren't in immediate danger, that experience exposed my husband and myself to trauma. I know of parents who have spent many weeks with their newborn baby in NICU, and I know of parents who have spent many weeks only to watch their baby die. I can't begin to imagine the trauma and sadness and loss. I was lucky and grateful to be able to take my healthy baby home with me, but the experience stayed with me. Spending so much time surrounded by sick and vulnerable babies made me lose a bit of perspective. The vulnerability

I saw in my baby was so intense that I became frightened to leave the house in case something terrible happened.

My personal experience

My second baby was born at the beginning of the pandemic. All the news about the virus made the world seem even more unsafe. It was harder to switch off from dangers and relax. Whenever we left the house, I felt so afraid that my toddler would fall into a river or a pond and drown, or fall and hurt himself. This fear manifested as anger and shouting. 'Don't run! Stay away from that river! Stay away from that dog!' If my son wasn't paying attention or was taking a risk (typical for a three-year-old), I would feel intense rage coursing through me. All this anger I was feeling caused us all so much stress. Then I realised I was in a trauma response again. I worked through this with an EMDR therapist and now I can leave the house feeling safe and calm. I'm still a little nervous that my boy will fall into a duck pond, but at least I know I can jump in and save him.

When we become mothers, we are hardwired to assess risk, and we feel the lack of safety in the world intimately. Anger can be a response to when we feel unsafe or feel our children are in danger. We feel angry with our children when we are scared that they are going to get hurt.

Your inner child

Angry inner child

Your inner child is an expression of your child self and the experiences your child self contains. If your inner child is still wounded from childhood trauma, you need to acknowledge and heal your inner child. As well as trauma, it's helpful to reflect on how your inner child experienced anger and other emotions. Your inner child will reveal these answers. One mother I spoke to said that her mother never outwardly expressed her anger, but would silently rage while doing the housework. Another mother said that expressions of anger and frustrations around the house were standard in her family. Later in the book, I have provided an inner child meditation to learn to tune into your inner child and learn more about your maternal anger.

Journal Prompt

- Growing up, how was anger expressed?
- What did anger mean to you?
- What did you learn about anger from your parents?
- Were there any angry outbursts or did anger manifest in a more silent rage?
- Were you afraid of anger growing up?
- Were you comfortable around bursts of emotional energy?

Motherhood as a trigger

Trauma doesn't always start in childhood. It can start during the process and journey of becoming a mother. The mother of an adopted two-year-old girl said, 'When I saw my daughter's distress, it woke up my distress. I was so sensitive. I was sensitive to everything. The two of us started our relationship in a trauma response.'

The process of conceiving can be traumatic in itself for various reasons, for instance, if you suffered miscarriages, went through intrusive fertility procedures or if your partner left you or cheated on you in pregnancy.

Pregnant women are more vulnerable to trauma. The hormonal changes we experience and the profound knowledge that we are growing a child means we are more sensitive to our environment and other people. The changes in our bodies can be traumatic as we may start to feel out of control, and this can continue during labour and birth. Sometimes this trauma can manifest as anger. Women can feel angry that their partner isn't going through the same physical and hormonal changes, the same pain or experience. Motherhood can trigger us in so many ways. The mother of a two-year-old girl says:

'No one warns mums how easily anger can be triggered as a parent. When you are with your child and alone, and you feel angry, no one tells you how to manage it or release it differently.'

Our relationship with our child can be a trigger. Certain personality traits, sounds they make, expressions on their face or how they touch you can be a trigger. A mother may then rage at their child and not have any idea why they are so angry. The mother of a twelve-year-old says:

'You know you have been triggered when you have this over-the-top reaction – an explosive reaction that seems to come out of nowhere. You are no longer you. You have gone into survival mode. You are functioning from a different place and fighting for your life.'

An exploration of trauma-induced anger

The situation

I worked with a new mum for eight weeks. She came to me feeling overwhelmed and tearful. She said she felt she was bonding with her baby, but also often felt short-tempered and angry. She often found herself snapping at her partner and breaking down in tears. She also felt disconnected at times, as if she was living life underneath a glass bell jar. She was concerned she had postnatal depression and didn't know what to do.

The therapy

I didn't want to pathologise my client by labelling her with postnatal depression. Instead, I explored closely, and without judgement, her experience of her birth and the first few weeks of being a new mum.

- How had she experienced the birth?
- What support was she getting?
- How did she manage her feelings before she became a mother?

My client revealed that she had suffered the loss of her mother a week before she gave birth. She was close to her mother and looking forward to sharing the experience of motherhood and having her much-needed support. It became clear to both of us that beneath her anger was grief. We gave space to the grief, anger and pain. Gently, we processed these emotions together with compassion.

The result

After a few sessions, my client started to feel less overwhelmed. Understanding that her feelings were due to grief, not her fault, and that she 'wasn't going mad' made them easier to navigate. She felt much more present with her baby and supported by her partner, who communicated with her better after realising what she was going through.

Many mothers I spoke to want to feel more confident in unpicking their triggers to maternal anger and rage. I want mums to recognise when they are triggered around their children and create a unique, self-soothing toolbox to have at hand. The next chapter explores what we can do when we are triggered (especially from trauma), how we can ground ourselves, and how we can heal from the pain of trauma so we choose our response instead of responding from a place of rage.

Journal Prompt

- What feelings, thoughts and memories did this chapter provoke in you?
- Write them down and then try and create a narrative around your childhood story and your story now as a mother.

Summary

Discovering and understanding maternal anger from the perspective of exposure to trauma is essential. While we can't expect our children to see the bigger picture, it is helpful for us as mothers to see trauma as part of our bigger picture. This perspective will make us less vulnerable to anger. Understanding our trauma history can enable us to unpick and reduce our trauma triggers. It may also give us insight into the anger of those around us if we understand their trauma history. What is essential is approaching trauma and the impact on you as a mother with compassion, gentleness and healing. If you feel trauma is underneath your maternal rage, then please reach out to a trauma-informed therapist.

FOUR

Navigating Maternal Rage Triggers

In this chapter, I explore trauma-informed tools and techniques in detail to help you navigate trauma triggers and moments of maternal anger and rage. If you can sense the difference between being triggered and being angry because the situation calls for anger, you will have more confidence and awareness to navigate these complex emotions. I hope you can develop a box of tools that can help you and that are unique to your situation.

Not everything will work. Some days you will need one type of tool more than another, and some days you may need to just survive. Consider these suggestions as offerings of support and not another thing that you 'need to do'. If any of them make your life harder rather than more manageable, then try something else. The idea is to give you strength, energy and compassionate support. They are not a stick to beat yourself with, so take it slowly and be gentle with yourself.

What can trigger maternal rage?

A trauma trigger is when a present experience reminds you of something that happened in the past, and you suddenly feel as if that past event is happening again. Your body and mind react as if you are in danger even though you are safe. A trigger can also be when a present experience triggers intense feelings which aren't just about what is going on. Human beings are meaning-makers. Everyday experiences can become heavy with the meanings we attribute.

Trauma isn't always a catalyst to a trigger. Sometimes, we create meaning and assumptions that compound how we react. That meaning, assumption or belief can be painful and can then make us angry in response to that pain. That is why it is helpful to approach intense feelings such as anger with a sense of curiosity. What am I making of this moment that makes me so angry? What are my thoughts, beliefs and assumptions here?

There is not enough scope for me to discuss every experience a mother may face so if your experience isn't mentioned here, please remember that it is still valid.

When speaking to mothers about what triggers maternal rage and anger, I found a lot of common ground. Similar themes kept emerging, which I have attempted to summarise. The more common themes seem to be when mothers feel that no one is listening. The mother is ignored and it feels as if their voice doesn't matter. Feeling unheard and ignored can be a massive trigger for anger. Our values and sense of self can feel annihilated.

Another theme is feeling incapable when a child turns down options around food and activities. As mothers, we try to negotiate with our children. We don't want to force them to eat or do something they don't want to do, but at the same time, we understand that our children need to eat healthily or do activities that are good for them. We can feel powerless when we engage with our children and try and convince them to eat their broccoli or put away the iPad. Feeling powerless triggers anger.

Other triggers for anger include whingeing and complaining, insults and bad behaviour, arguments, siblings fighting, and when our partners are not pulling their weight and not supporting decisions. Stressful situations such as teething, sleep training, potty training, feeding refusals, bullying at school, exams and tests and tantrums also provoke anger. Many of these situations would make anyone feel out of control and powerless, and if feeling out of control and powerless has a painful echo for you, it will leave you vulnerable to anger and rage. All these situations can trigger our anger without having been exposed to much trauma in our lives. Although it is hard to differentiate between what is or isn't based on trauma, we can take some of our control back. Feeling powerless is often a strong indication that we have been triggered. Feeling powerless means our nervous system is indicating we are in danger or being threatened. Hatty, mother of a six-year-old boy, says:

'I find that I am not particularly angry in general. It will be specific situations where I get angry. My anger flares up around anxiety and when I feel like I am trapped either physically or emotionally.'

The window of tolerance

Have you ever wondered why some days you can feel bad-tempered, agitated and snappy and other days you can feel a bit spaced-out and numb? These responses could be because you are outside of your window of tolerance. The window of tolerance is a concept that was introduced by clinical psychiatrist Dr Daniel Siegel.[9] It refers to an optimal state of functioning for our nervous system. Ideally, we should all be functioning from within our window of toler-

---

9   D Siegel, *The Developing Mind: How relationships and the brain interact to shape who we are* (Second ed, New York: The Guilford Press, 2012)

ance, but those who have been exposed to trauma can struggle to stay within the window of tolerance.

When we are within our window of tolerance, we can tolerate the everyday ebb and flow and ups and downs that life throws at us. As mothers, when we have days that seem less challenging to us and we feel calm and grounded, we function within the window of tolerance. Hurt, pain, anxiety and anger will bring us to the edge of our window. When this happens, we need to utilise strategies to keep us within the window.

Feeling burnt out, exhausted, sad and shut down can bring you out of the window of tolerance. When we experience adversity through trauma, this drastically disrupts our nervous system. Our window of tolerance becomes smaller, our senses are heightened, our experiences are intensified, and our self-soothing strategies will be less accessible to us. When your maternal anger gets powerful, you may be moving out of your window of tolerance. When we come out of our window of tolerance, we either go into hyperarousal or hypo-arousal.

Hyperarousal is characterised by:

- Excessive energy

- Anxiety

- Panic

- Hypervigilance

- Difficulty relaxing
- Difficulty sleeping
- Difficulty digesting food
- Rage and hostility

Hypo-arousal is characterised by:

- Exhaustion
- Depression
- Being zoned out
- Numb
- Frozen

These reactions are not something you can choose. Mums need to know about this to understand what is going on when they are feeling intense feelings. When you feel spaced out and exhausted, you can utilise strategies to bring you back inside your window. When you feel short-tempered and cross, you can utilise strategies that calm your nervous system down and reduce emotional outbursts around your children.

Rage in a hyperarousal state

Monica, a young mother I spoke to, described how she raged around her children. Her reactions to annoying behaviour felt out of proportion and uncontrolled. She would go from loving to livid in seconds. Afterwards, she felt such guilt for reacting in this way. Her mother was often hostile, her anger uncontained, and the thought of being like that was unbearable to her. She needed to get a handle on her rage. Every morning she woke up promising herself that she wouldn't snap or shout at her child.

When Monica realised that her reaction was because she was out of her window of tolerance and was a trauma response possibly created through her own experience of her hostile mother, she was able to take back control. Taking back control is vital to trauma survivors as their control has been taken away profoundly. Knowing what was going on made it seem less scary. It also encouraged her to start the healing process of her childhood trauma. After working through her trauma, she noticed less rage and hostility around her children (and herself).

What do I do when I am triggered?

If you find yourself triggered as a parent, it is crucial to have a safety plan. You can even create a physical self-soothing first aid kit to have nearby for moments when it feels too intense and overwhelming. Dan Siegel coined a phrase: 'Name it to tame it'. When triggered, we need to:

- Recognise
- Accept

- Tolerate
- Validate

Next time you notice yourself feeling anger (even if it is low-level frustration), try following the steps below:

1. Pause.

2. Get into the present moment.

3. Give the anger recognition.

4. Give it acceptance.

5. Allow it to be.

6. Validate the anger.

Practise this each time you feel anger. Self-awareness practices can help you when you are triggered. The more aware you are, the more you will notice the specific things that trigger your anger. Many of the mothers I spoke to said that, essentially, a feeling of powerlessness triggered their anger. It is helpful for you to know what triggers you. Isobel, mother of a four-year-old girl, says:

> 'I tend to get into a rage when I have tried everything to get my child to do something, and until they do that thing, I am stuck and can't get on with the things I need to do. Cleaning their teeth, getting undressed and then dressed in their pyjamas. I try to be calm

and use all the tricks, but sometimes it enrages me that they just won't do what they are told. I find it very frustrating.'

When do you feel rage the most in your day? Is it first thing in the morning when you've not had a chance to drink a coffee or have space for breakfast, exercise and even two minutes to shower and use the bathroom? I took my morning routine for granted before having children. I would wake up slowly, drink coffee in bed, have a shower in my own time and listen to music or the news on the radio then make breakfast. I would do a morning meditation and yoga practice or rush to the gym. I could access an early morning twelve-step group if I needed to check in and share. Now, my morning routine is completely different, and it makes me angry. I get more frustrated in the mornings than at any other time of the day. Mornings now feel stressful – like I'm constantly moving from one thing to the next without pause for breath, right from the moment I wake up. Showers are rushed, going to the toilet is rushed and eating breakfast is rushed. Mornings are now accompanied by the sounds of nursery rhymes and Disney songs. But I can also remember that I don't always have to immediately respond to the demands of my children and I can allow myself a little bit more time on each activity.

I don't need to explain to you how fraught mornings can be. As a mother, mornings can be triggering, especially if the kids don't 'play ball'. One mother I spoke to said that she needs a cup of coffee first thing in the morning before she can begin her day of parenting her two boys. She feels lucky that her wife works from home so she is able to have that space to drink her coffee and shower in peace. Then, once her wife needs to step into her home office at 9 am, she is energised and ready to start the day. One mother noticed she is more vulnerable to being triggered if she doesn't get this morning space. For other mothers, they feel they are more triggered when they are outside the home with their children and feel they have an audience for their parenting. For many parents, it is the evening, when they are tired and low in energy, that they are more likely to be on a short fuse. It is worth keeping note of when you are at your most short-tempered.

- What time of the day is it?
- Are you inside the house or in a public space?
- Are you travelling?

Getting back into your window of tolerance

Once you've applied recognition, acceptance, tolerance and validation to as many of your rage triggers as you're able to, you can concentrate on working towards getting back into your window of tolerance. The exercises below are easy to do and can assist you with this – choose those that you feel most comfortable with:

- **Smell:** The smell of essential oils, herbal tea, scented candles and your favourite food and drink (mine is coffee and bread).

- **Taste:** Soothing tastes such as honey and ginger and stimulating tastes such as lemon and chilli.

- **Sound:** Create your own energising or soothing playlists. The sounds of birdsong and water are both soothing. The Calm app (www.calm.com) has some lovely sounds to calm you down.

- **Touch:** Soft toy, blanket, silk or woollen scarfs, ice, standing on grass or in the sand. (Next time you take your children to the sandpit, put your bare feet in the sand, close your eyes for a moment and pretend you are on a beach.)

- **Visual:** Look around the room and notice the colours. Name five things in the colour blue. Imagine a safe and calm image (I imagine a beach at sunset).

- **Voice:** Singing, growling or shouting.

- **Body:** Breathing (take five deep breaths or blow bubbles), yoga positions (yoga nidra is a good calming position), mindfulness meditations.

What helps to ground you?

Grounding techniques

The fastest way to ground yourself is to clap your hands and stamp your feet (easily done around children). I will explain how to accept and listen to your anger and communicate it differently later in the book but before we begin making space for anger, here are a few grounding exercises and safe place exercises to keep you in your window of tolerance. The more you practise these, the more confident you will feel in creating space for your anger. I have based these exercises on EMDR and Laura Parnell's book *A Therapist's Guide to EMDR*.[10]

Safe space exercise

Sit in a comfortable, relaxed manner with your legs un-crossed and hands gently resting on your knees. Close your eyes and take a few deep breaths. In your mind, slowly walk down a flight of stairs with ten steps. As you take each step, take a deep breath and relax into your body more profoundly and deeper with each step. Imagine a real place at the bottom of the steps where you feel your most grounded and relaxed. When you feel grounded and calm, do some slow butterfly taps. Imagine the sounds, the smells, the colours. What can you see, and how do you feel? Then slowly walk back up the steps and open your eyes. Practise this exercise every day.

(Butterfly taps technique: Cross your arms over your chest, so that the tip of the middle finger from each hand is placed below the collarbone. Your hand and fingers should be as vertical as possible, so that the fingers point towards the neck and not towards the arms. Your eyes can be closed, or partially closed. Alternate the movement of your hands, like the flapping wings of a butterfly; let your hands move freely. Aim

---

10 L Parnell, *A Therapist's Guide to EMDR: Tools and techniques for successful treatment* (WW Norton & Company, First ed, January 2007)

to breathe slowly and deeply while you observe what is going on through your mind and body.)[11]

Resources exercise

My **nurturer** is: (Think of a person in your life or someone from history or popular culture who represents nurturing; the person you would go to when you need nurturing.)

My **wise person** is: (Think of a person in your life or someone from history or popular culture who represents wisdom; the person you would go to when you need wisdom.)

My **protector** is: (Think of a person in your life or someone from history or popular culture who represents protection; the person you would go to when you need protection.)

Imagine these three people sitting with you in your safe space. Do slow butterfly taps when thinking of the protection, the wisdom and the nurturing experience of these people while in your safe, grounded space.

The four elements exercise

Use the four elements to ground yourself.

---

11   Crowe Associates Ltd, 'Butterfly Hug – a self-directed EMDR method' (Crowe Associates Ltd, no date), www.crowe-associates.co.uk/psychotherapy/butterfly-hug-method, accessed 28 August 2021

Earth is about grounding yourself and having a sense of safety in the present moment. Give yourself a moment to ground yourself by placing both feet on the ground. If possible, step outside on the grass in bare feet. Notice the sensation of the ground supporting you. Notice what is around you: can you see five things the colour of blue?

Air is about how we bring breath into the body. Breathing can help centre you and bring you into your body. Breathing can help you notice how your body is in this moment and help reduce any tension. Breathe in through your nose as you count four seconds and breathe out through your mouth as you count four seconds.

Water is to help you feel calm and controlled. Water switches on the relaxation response in your mind by putting saliva in your mouth. When you are anxious or stressed, your mouth often dries because part of the stress emergence response is to shut off the digestion system. When you start making saliva, you switch your digestion and the relaxation response on again. Mindfully chewing gum or drinking tea or cold water will switch on your digestion system, and the sensation of water in your mouth will bring you a sense of calm and control.

Fire is about firing up your imagination. Bring up an image of your safe place or any memory where you feel good about yourself. Indulge in that memory.

You can ground yourself further by:

- Putting cream or oil on your skin

- Throwing / kicking a ball with your child

- Going outside and noticing the trees and grass and sky

- Looking out the window and counting how many birds you see

- Taking the children to a nearby farm to feed and pet some animals

- Listening, dancing and singing to music

It is worth mentioning that you can do a lot of healing and transformative grounding work to reduce your rage triggers, but take notice if you keep putting yourself back into triggering situations. Once grounded, you may become easily re-triggered if you then go and spend time with unsafe people or in an unsafe situation. It is much harder to avoid if it's your child or your partner triggering you, but it can be worth digging deeper with EMDR or therapy to get to the root trigger and try to heal from that so the present triggers are reduced.

For example, a mother may be triggered by the sound of her baby crying. That particular trigger could be because of hormones, because the crying taps into our feeling of powerlessness, or because we are genetically hardwired to respond to our baby crying. If we find the sound irritating and distracting, we may associate the distress with hurt, pain, abuse or danger. Sometimes the sound of a baby crying can increase our cortisol levels. We are then triggered when our brain becomes overwhelmed; we fall out of our window of tolerance and may go into fight, flight, freeze or fawn mode. If we fly into a rage, we have gone into fight mode. Babies cry a lot. It doesn't mean that they are in pain, danger or being abused, but if our brain makes that connection it is hard to respond differently. It is also entirely possible to break that connection and create a new perspective and experience where the sound of our baby crying simply means our baby is hungry or tired. We are in control and have the power to do something about it. It is worth getting to know your triggers and noticing your autonomy around triggers.

Journaling can be incredibly grounding and therapeutic in itself. Keep a diary of your triggers, how you responded to them, what grounding exercises you did and if they helped. Use the following questions as prompts.

Journal Prompt

- Do you unknowingly always find yourself in situations that are triggering?
- Do you ground yourself and then undo the work by consuming too much caffeine, alcohol or sugar?

- Do you speak to toxic people in your life who then make you doubt yourself or have negative ways of behaving that put you out of our window of tolerance?

Summary

Maternal anger can be a response to being triggered. Rage and anger can be a sign you have come out of your window of tolerance or moving towards the edges of your window. Through self-awareness exercises and grounding techniques, we can learn to stay within the window and be less vulnerable to triggers.

FIVE

Tuning Into Anger

'Anybody can become angry – that is easy... but to be angry with the right person and to the right amount, and at the right time, and for the right purpose, and in the right way – this is not within everybody's power and is not easy.'[12]
— Aristotle

Anger contains vital messages for us as mothers. If we don't make space for anger, it can become internally toxic if we continue to suppress it. Anger needs to be given space the same way we make space for joy and happiness. To be more attuned to the ebb and flow of anger and the messages contained within, we need to make space for it. The more attuned you

---

12 Aristotle, *Nicomachean Ethics*, (Volume XIX) (Harvard University Press, Second edn, 1934)

are to your emotions, the less likely they are to sneak up on you. Even if they take you by surprise, you will tolerate your emotions and notice when you shift in and out of different emotional states.

It is worth remembering that you are not your thoughts and you are not your emotions. Making space for anger helps you reflect upon the anger, and anger reflected upon is more likely to be expressed constructively and healthily. When anger is unreflected, it is more likely to come out as rage. It is OK to make space for rage and anger as long as that rage isn't going to harm you or others.

Once we make space for our anger, we can also model how to be angry for our daughters. One mother I spoke to said she sees her nine-year-old daughter's discomfort in being angry and her internal struggle to express anger, while her son doesn't seem to have that struggle and is quickly expressive with his anger.

How do we make space for anger?

The more we allow ourselves as women and mothers to make space for anger, the more we can reclaim the narrative around anger. Many of the mothers I spoke to said that they felt a sense of shame around their anger. The shame around anger seems to be about women not feeling allowed to be angry. Expressing anger is often seen as a woman being bossy, crazy, out of control, a nag or a shrew. This attitude is society's way of discouraging the expression of anger. We need to make space for women to understand the strength and the power behind expressing their anger.

You may think that you are making space for anger in your life simply by losing your temper (and this may seem more than enough, thank you!). Why make space for something you are trying to reduce?

Correctly making space for anger won't make you angrier. In fact, it will make you less angry. When you make space for anger, you let go of it; the anger changes form and you have room to breathe. It becomes lighter. When you don't make space for anger, only you will suffer from the suffocating quality of suppressed rage. To make space for anger (or any intense emotion), you need to feel safe and grounded. Please use the grounding techniques in the previous chapter before and after any time spent making space for anger or develop your own techniques by researching what works for you. Ideally, you should also work with a therapist to give you a space to process what comes out of spending time with anger. I appreciate that not everyone has the time or the resources for therapy, but if you can access therapy, I encourage you to try it.

Making space for anger means practising being aware of the difference in your mind and body between when you feel grounded, when you are feeling intense anger, and when you return to feeling grounded again.

I use the word 'practise' because it takes practice to make space for anger and to stay angry. I found that doing this practice within the safely contained relationship with a therapist was a profound experience. I am not just telling you this because I am a therapist. I appreciate the courage it takes to sit with your anger when you have always believed anger as being something to fear or that others will find unacceptable. Sitting with another person who accepts your anger and can withstand it was profoundly therapeutic for me.

How do we practise mindfulness around anger?

Mindfulness is a respectful and gentle way to make space for our anger. Mindfulness is *knowing what is going on inside and outside of ourselves, moment by moment.* Mindfulness is about fostering an awareness of everything going on for us: every thought, sensation, feeling and bodily experience. Mindfulness will help you to make space for your anger safely and compassionately. By being aware of what is going on for yourself moment to moment with an attitude of curiosity rather than judgement, you will learn to attune to your anger and the messages it brings and inform your thinking and impact your feelings. It will help you to understand how your anger is changing the way you are relating and communicating. This simple act of self-awareness can give you pause to stop, breathe and choose if you wish to react, communicate and relate differently. Mindfulness essentially empowers you to recognise your embodied and somatic experiences, the world around you, and the interplay between you and people, places, and things.

The following steps will assist you practise mindful meditation. Try and maintain a non-judgemental and curious approach about it:

1. Choose a time when you won't be disturbed.

2. Choose a time when you are feeling safe, grounded and calm.

3. Sit or lie down in a comfortable position and allow your body to settle.

4. Take ten deep breaths (in through your nose and out through your mouth).

5. Gently close your eyes.

6. Mentally scan your body.

7. Do you notice any tension in your body?

8. Be curious, gentle and compassionate about the tension:

    – What feeling or sensation is the tension?

    – Is there a shape or an image to the tension?

    – Does your body feel numb or hollow?

- When you are ready, take a few more deep breaths and wriggle your fingers and toes.

- Open your eyes and look around the room.

Once you start making space for anger, you can allow yourself to feel the anger without it hijacking you. You will begin to notice how it impacts your thoughts and feelings and your views about yourself and the world. Making space for anger through mindfulness can help you notice how anger manifests in your thoughts:

- Have your thoughts become black and white?

- More certain?

- Are they feeding into new thoughts, building a picture or an argument to solidify why you are angry?

- Are your thoughts encouraging the anger even if they aren't based on fact?

- Are your thoughts about the past, present or future?

When we are in our anger, it is hard for us to cognitively and emotionally be in the present situation. Our minds and emotions may take us somewhere to the past or the future. Future thoughts may be triggering your anger, for example:

- 'He isn't going to sleep tonight again and I desperately need sleep.'

- 'He isn't going to help me when he gets home from work. He'll just sit and watch TV while I do everything.'

- 'She won't eat her dinner again.'

These things haven't happened yet, but you are already feeling angry about them. Giving space to your anger allows you to pause and think about if a situation is going to happen. The statements in the example suggest that you don't have control. Instead, consider what control you *do* have. I find The Serenity Prayer from the Alcoholics Anonymous twelve-step programme instrumental in moments like this: 'Grant me the serenity to accept the things I cannot change, courage to change the things I can, and the wisdom to know the difference.'[13]

Journal Prompt

If it's a past thought that is making you angry, spend some time reflecting upon and writing down all the events and situations in the past that have made you angry since you became a mother. Apply the four-step approach to this past anger (recognise, accept, tolerate and validate) and notice what happens. Do you still feel angry? Is there anything you can do about it? Do you need to talk it out with someone?

---

13   B Wilson, *Alcoholics Anonymous: The story of how many thousands of men and women have recovered from alcoholism* (New York: Alcoholics Anonymous World Services, 1976)

When making space for something going on in the present moment, ask yourself, 'What it is that is making me angry? What can I change in the present moment, and what can I accept?'

The more you make space for your anger through practising mindfulness, the more you can choose how you engage with those angry thoughts. Mindfulness can stop you from getting too caught up and lost in your anger. Remember, you don't have to believe everything you think.

Any time you spend with your emotions, please meditate in a safe space before and afterwards. Meditation will keep you grounded and confident to withstand complex emotions. You can practise mindfulness throughout the day. Once you recognise your anger by changing your thoughts and feelings, you can regularly check in on it. You do not have to do anything other than notice it. How intense is it? Mindfulness can help you figure out what times in the day your anger is the most and least intense. Do you wake up feeling angry? Do you wake up thinking angry thoughts? Who are you with when you are angry? Who are you with when your thoughts seem calm? You may think that you don't have time to be mindful, but remember that it doesn't have to take up much time and it actually creates space for you when you don't have any.

How to find time to practise mindfulness:

- Walking with your baby in the buggy. Notice the trees, the sky, the clouds, the weather and the sounds around you.

- Feeding your baby can be a significant downtime to do an internal check on what is going on for you. Scan your body.

- Ask someone else to look after your children and do a mindfulness exercise for the first three minutes you have to yourself. You will feel noticeably calmer for the rest of the time you have to yourself.

- Lying in bed at night. My bedtime meditations seem to help me sleep more soundly.

- Meditations first thing in the morning. Before you pick up your phone, do a five-minute body scan (or a twenty-minute meditation if your routine allows you this luxury).

- When you drop your children off at school, before you do anything else, do a five-minute body scan in your car, or on public transport, or as you walk home.

- Listen to relaxing, soothing music while you're driving. Make a playlist of songs that you find calming.

Making space for your angry inner child

Your inner child contains so much wisdom; she knows everything about you and has experienced everything you have experienced. You, as a child, matter so much. Your inner child may well be carrying any grief and shame from childhood. Getting in touch with your inner child and listening to what she has to say can tell you a profound amount about your maternal anger and your relationship with your children. Your inner child might be feeling angry if you weren't loved and valued enough as a child. Suppose you grew up in a chaotic family environment. On some level, you as a child will be holding on to a lot of anger around that. Even if you had the most beautiful childhood, there will be elements of your childhood that will have caused some pain, disruption and anger. You may be surprised at how much truth your inner child is holding.

Sometimes, when we are angry around our children, it is our inner child that is angry. She may feel something is unfair and feels she must protest. She may want attention. Simply listening to her can be all the nurturing and care she needs. If you feel that sitting and listening to your inner child could be triggering, please bookend the experience with grounding, meditation and speaking to a trusted friend or therapist.

Inner child meditation

Get into a comfortable position where you won't be disturbed. Close your eyes and take some deep breaths, relaxing your body further and further with each breath. Now imagine your childhood home. Notice the house, notice the front door, notice the colour and the size and shape of it. Go up to the front door and knock. Imagine your child self opening the front door. How old is she? What is she wearing? Is she happy to see you? What is her mood?

Take her hand and walk inside the house. How do you feel as you walk into the house? Is the house quiet and calm, or is it noisy and full of people? Allow your child self to take you upstairs into her bedroom. Notice the bedroom. Is it tidy, or chaotic and messy? Sit with her on the bed. What is she doing? Does she start playing? What would you like to say to her? What would it be like to give her a hug and some affection? Notice what it is like to do that. Can you spend some time with her? Now thank her for spending time with you and let her walk you outside of the house. Say goodbye and then open your eyes.

Give yourself slow butterfly taps and take five deep breaths. Notice how you feel now compared to before you did the meditation.

Anger can also be the rebellious inner teen trying to get their needs heard and assert their boundaries. They are rebelling against perceived authority. Sometimes when we make space for anger, what emerges is our angry inner teen. I found that when I became pregnant the second time around. I felt like a moody teenager going through puberty. When I had been a moody teenager going through puberty, I had often felt that my voice wasn't being heard, and like most teenagers, I'd wanted to rebel against authority. Our inner teenagers may still want to rebel against authority. I have noticed with my child that we can often get into a power struggle for authority. The other day I snapped at him and said, 'You are not the boss; I am the boss!' He was quiet for a moment and then asked me what a boss was. He didn't even understand the concept, but in that moment I was angry when I felt my authority and voice being taken away and felt the struggle for authority with my three-year-old. That may sound ridiculous, or it may be highly relatable. Either way, do make space to listen to your rebellious inner teen as well as your inner child. It is also worthwhile taking the time to internally reflect upon a time or times in your life when you were your most angry. Is that version of yourself stuck in that anger and sometimes emerging in the present?

Other, more embodied ways we can get in touch with anger is through yoga and Qi Gong. I had a beautiful healing experience once after a yoga session. We were in the resting pose and a dark room with calming music, and the yoga teacher was taking us through a meditation. Suddenly I heard this angry voice within myself, a voice that seemed to come from the core of who I was. The voice said loudly and clearly, with assertion (and yes, with anger), 'You deserve to be loved better.'

Journal Prompt

Write a letter to your inner child and rebellious inner teen. Invite dialogue with no purpose other than to talk and listen, validate and potentially heal.

Summary

Hopefully this chapter has given you permission to stop and sit with your anger and develop a new relationship with anger. The exercises should help you to understand your anger better and to tolerate it more. The intention is that the next time anger ungrounds you, you can work your way back to feeling grounded again. Sitting with your anger while ungrounded possibly won't work, so try this when you are in a stable place. When overwhelmed with anger, walk away, take a few breaths to regulate yourself, then sit with what happened at a later time. Keep writing your experience down.

SIX

Communication And Repair

At this point in the maternal anger roadmap, you should have a clearer understanding of maternal anger and the role, purpose and value of anger. You will also have a sense of how traumatic experiences from childhood can exacerbate and trigger maternal anger and how motherhood itself can be a trigger to maternal anger. If you have tried out a few grounding exercises and journal prompts and used mindfulness and meditation to make space for your anger and tuned into it, hopefully you are feeling a bit calmer as a parent and are developing a new relationship with your maternal anger.

How do we communicate our anger? When we are angry, something isn't right, or something isn't working for us, we need to say, 'This is not OK.' It is hard, because anger can impact communication. This chapter looks at how maternal anger impacts communication and how we can speak our truth and be heard when we are angry. It also looks at repair after rupture.

Maternal anger and communication

How easy do you find it to speak when you are angry? I have always found it difficult to speak when I am angry. For me, anger can be an acidic and bitter taste in my mouth. Speaking when angry, even if I am not shouting, hurts my throat. It has taken practice for me to be able to speak clearly and assertively when I am angry. Being angry and speaking my truth without tears and apology has taken compassion and self-repair.

Other mothers I spoke to said that they have never had a problem with being angry and communicating that anger. They were more confident and felt more validated in expressing their anger. One mother that I spoke to said that she often cried when she was angry, which frustrated her as it made her feel weak and vulnerable. She wanted to show her anger with more strength and conviction. Crying when you are angry is common for women and shows what a painful and complex energy anger is.

When angry, thinking becomes black and white and less fluid and creative. This profoundly impacts communication. When angry, your tone of voice changes; you may sound harsher and louder, or may be quieter and a bit more measured and strained. Sometimes, we may spit out the words as if we are spitting out the poison behind our anger. Our choice of words will be different depending on our mood, and with anger, we may choose to swear or use language which has blame and shaming undertones. We may not even notice how differently we speak when we are angry or realise that we feel angry through our words and tone.

Your children are always in tune with you and will notice how you communicate when you are angry. Do you tend to use specific words in specific ways? Do you feel confident to communicate your anger effectively? How do you communicate your anger? Emma, a single mother of three teenagers, says:

> 'When my anger is uncontained, I start shouting. I sound like my father, who shouted a lot when I was a child. What usually gets me angry is when I see the boys fighting, and sometimes it looks like they are going to hurt each other. Without their father being around and me having to deal with everything, I find dealing with this situation the hardest. My energy matches the male energy in the room. I get louder, and they feed off me and they get louder, and I just want to swear at them.'

Other ways we may communicate when angry:

- Rolling our eyes
- Gestures
- Facial expressions
- Tone of voice
- Silence
- Switching off and not being present

When you are angry, your perspective shifts. You may not be able to think through the nuances of a situation with calmness and clarity like you would, for instance, first thing in the morning when you're in a good mood, the sun is shining, and you've just had a coffee and a full night's sleep. You will naturally also communicate differently when angry compared to when you're calm. Ideally, you'd like to speak calmly and gently at all times, but this isn't always possible. The power you have in this situation is being aware of your tone, language and body language.

When I am angry around my children, there is a part of me that wants them to know that I am angry. I think it's the part of me that wants to prove to the room that I have power, that I have freedom and choices, and that my identity, voice and needs matter. In the same way, my children also need to express this. On the rare occasions when I do shout, I feel powerful. I feel my strength, and it feels good in that moment, but I know it isn't a good or fair experience for my children. The need to express me is *my* need – the children don't get anything from it. There will be situations when my children make me angry, but I need to own my anger around them. The way I communicate will become louder and harsher, but it is still contained and I am still in control.

Ideally, when we communicate anger around our children, we aim to harmonise with our emotions and to own our feelings. It is an excellent gift to our children to model anger with as much authenticity as possible in a non-threatening way. Denying you are angry when you are is confusing. Being angry and shouting over something which isn't the situation you are angry about is also confusing. Children are so tuned into our moods that they will notice when we are not in harmony with our emotions.

We are modelling how to handle our emotions for our children all the time. That is why engaging in the process of making space for your anger and tuning in to know why you are angry is so essential. That way, it is easier for you to own and contain your anger and be in harmony with your emotions. You are no longer having a battle with how you are feeling or suppressing it, but allowing your authentic self to be heard.

Communicating to your child that you are angry is OK, as children can learn from this, but make space for and understand your anger before you communicate it. Communicate from a place of empathy and compassion rather than from a place of shame and blame. Children appreciate honesty and clarity. It helps them to understand what has happened and to process it in their way. It can enable learning about relationships, but there is a risk that it can be damaging if the anger communication is done from a place of unreflected rage. Never blame your child for your anger. Try to own your anger around your child even while explaining it. Normalising anger without deflection and blame can make it non-threatening for your child.

Journal Prompt

- Growing up, how did people communicate their anger around you?
- How do you and your partner communicate anger?

Mothers in conflict

Conflict is defined as a state of opposition, disagreement or incompatibility between two or more people or groups of people, characterised by physical violence. Conflicts are typically rooted in a clash of values, needs, interests or actions. Conflict is unavoidable. It is helpful to raise awareness of how we respond to conflict and the role we tend to play when there is conflict.

Anger and conflict are closely related. Often, to communicate our needs, values and boundaries underneath our anger, we need to engage in conflict. Not everyone will share the same values and needs as you and show the right amount of respect for your boundaries, so when you express your anger in this way, there may be a conflict. Mothers often feel their needs are not being met and that their boundaries are not being respected, making conflict entirely realistic and possible.

The Drama Triangle

The Drama Triangle was created in 1968[14] by Dr Karpman, a transactional analyst. It is a model which illustrates how conflict can arise and the roles we play in it. When we are in the drama triangle, the 'issue' that has created a conflict is not resolved. In the drama triangle, we play a role and react like characters in a play. We can get caught up in a script that can become increasingly familiar.

The Victim: The Victim's stance is 'poor me'. The Victim feels victimised, oppressed, helpless, hopeless, powerless, ashamed, and seems unable to make decisions, solve problems or achieve insight. If not being persecuted, the Victim will seek out a Persecutor and a Rescuer who will save the day and perpetuate the Victim's negative feelings.

---

14 S Karpman, *Fairy Tales and Script Drama Analysis* (1968), https://
karpmandramatriangle.com/pdf/DramaTriangle.pdf, accessed 26
August 2021

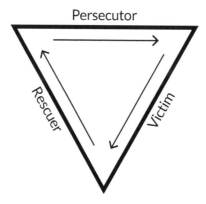

The Drama Triangle. Adapted from S Karpman's Drama Triangle[15]

The Rescuer: The Rescuer's line is, 'Let me help you.' The Rescuer, a classic enabler, feels guilty if they don't go to the rescue, yet the rescuing has adverse effects. It keeps the Victim dependent and gives the Victim permission to fail. The rewards derived from this rescue role are that the focus is taken off of the Rescuer. When they focus their energy on someone else, it enables them to ignore their anxiety and issues. This rescue role is also pivotal because their primary interest is avoiding their problems disguised as concern for the Victim's needs.

The Persecutor (aka Villain): The Persecutor insists, 'It's all your fault.' The Persecutor is controlling, blaming, critical, oppressive, angry, rigid and superior.

---

15 S Karpman, *A Game Free Life: The definitive book on the Drama Triangle and Compassion Triangle by the originator and author* (Drama Triangle Publications, January 2014)

Initially, a drama triangle arises when a person takes on the role of a Victim or Persecutor. This person feels the need to enlist other players into the conflict. As often happens, a rescuer is encouraged to enter the situation. These enlisted players take on roles of their own that are not static, and so various scenarios can occur. For example, the Victim might turn on the Rescuer, and the Rescuer then switches to persecuting.

Can you spot yourself in any of these roles? If you are in a conflict or power struggle that is not getting resolved and is increasing your maternal rage, please see where you fit in this drama triangle. It will then be clearer which behaviour you need to employ to help resolve the conflict in a respectful way, where rage won't get triggered.

The Winner's Triangle:
A way out of the Drama Triangle

Acey Choy published the Winner's Triangle[16] in 1990 as a therapeutic model for showing how to alter social transactions when entering a triangle at any of the three entry points. Choy recommends that anyone feeling like a victim think more about being vulnerable and caring. Anyone cast as a persecutor adopts an assertive posture, and anyone recruited to be a rescuer should react by being 'caring'.

---

16 A Choy, 'The Winner's Triangle' (*Transactional Analysis Journal*, Jan 1990), https://journals.sagepub.com/doi/10.1177/036215379002000105, accessed 26 August 2021

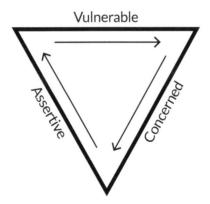

The Winner's Triangle. Adapted from A Choy's
'The Winner's Triangle'

Vulnerable: A victim should be encouraged to accept their vulnerability, to problem-solve and be more self-aware.

Assertive: A persecutor should be encouraged to ask for what they want and to be assertive, but not punishing.

Concerned: A rescuer should be encouraged to show concern and be caring, but not over-reach and problem-solve for others.

A way out of the drama triangle is to express vulnerability, be aware of your resources in getting your own needs met, focus on yourself and not do for others what they can do for themselves. *To express vulnerability means expressing how you genuinely feel.* For some mothers, this may feel threatening and uneasy. Modelling vulnerability is a beautiful gift to your children.

Another way we can express vulnerability is to step away from our ego and not make the situation about who is right or who is wrong. The rightness or wrongness doesn't matter. The more you cling to needing to be correct, the more the conflict will remain unresolved. Step out of that box.

The Persecutor can be assertive by using their energy to solve issues rather than blaming others for the problem and punishing or putting others down. Through being assertive, you can maintain your boundaries without stepping on other people's boundaries.

The Rescuer can move to being concerned by supporting the Victim's ability to solve the problem and refrain from doing everything for them. Caring allows the Victim to develop their own resources.

My personal experience

I was at home during the first pandemic lockdown when we could only go for one walk a day. My boys were eight weeks old and three years old. We had been stuck indoors and were all feeling a bit restless and grumpy. I had been desperate to go for a walk all day. At 3pm, once everyone had napped and eaten and was dressed, I ran upstairs to get ready. All I could hear from downstairs was crying, moaning and general noises of frustration and discontent.

I felt immediate rage. Here I was trying to be positive and energetic, persuading my family to go on a walk, which was the only thing we could do. I had been looking forward to this walk all day. Their lack of gratitude and unawareness of my plight upset me. Feeling the rage bursting within me, I stomped down the stairs. With tears in my eyes, I shouted, 'Just stop moaning!' There was immediate silence. My little boy looked at his daddy and said, 'Mummy wants you to stop moaning.' My husband looked at me, sighed, and said, 'Right, let's go then.'

I could see my husband was a bit anxious about going on the walk. People were not social distancing around us and that made him edgy. I knew he'd rather stay at home and keep us all safe. Rather than get annoyed, I approached the situation with compassion. We still went out for a walk, but I also understood my family's confusion and nerves over the pandemic. If I had said, 'OK, let's stay at home,' I would have been the Rescuer. If I had stayed in the place of blame and anger (how dare they ruin this walk for me), then I would have been the Persecutor. If I had stayed silent and upset that my family were not on board with going on a walk, I would have been the Victim. Immediately showing compassion after expressing my frustration changed the mood of the entire family.

Anger strengthens relationships. Conflicts, if managed well, can make people more intimate and more connected as they understand each other's values, needs and boundaries.

Speaking your truth when angry

Mothers must speak their truth when angry. Your truth as women and mothers needs to be heard. Our frustrations need to be witnessed and validated. Speaking our truth is also taking responsibility. There is an intriguing balancing act of communicating maternal anger around your children so your children can hear you without rupturing the relationship. You are not always going to get this right.

Some people struggle to communicate their anger when they are tuned in to the feelings of another. Sometimes we can be so empathic and understanding that we struggle to cause another person distress, but we can still learn to assert boundaries and communicate that we are unhappy with any behaviour when someone is hurting or having a tough time and vulnerable. Having a plan to communicate your anger around your children can give you something to fall back on in really fraught situations.

If you've done some work giving space to, and reflecting on, your anger by this point, you will be more familiar with your triggers and the next time you lose your temper around your child, it won't come as too much of a shock to you. I spoke with a mother who described herself as outspoken and direct. She expressed her feelings that anger is a necessary part of being a mother. Reflecting on her experience, she said:

> 'You can't paint everything a golden colour. There are shades of dark within motherhood. There are problems, and there will be times when you feel like the exorcist, and your head wants to start spinning. There will be times when your anger is very much there. Don't sugar-coat it.

> 'If my daughter does something that makes me angry and I swallow it, and then maybe the next time she does it, I swallow it again, then the third time she does it, my anger will come out at a ridiculous level that it shouldn't have gone to. I am very much for the approach of, the first time she does something wrong, I say, "I feel angry because you didn't listen, and you could have hurt yourself. It is very important that you listen to me so you can be safe."'

Anger is more potent if you speak honestly about the behaviour with the child and the impact the behaviour could have had (or did have). You can also take it further by ending the conversation with something positive such as, 'You're usually such a good listener, and I'm sure next time you will listen. I love you.' If they don't listen again, you can remind them that you have hope that they can listen and you are angry with them for not listening again. Remember to be angry with the behaviour and not the person. It's a tricky balance, but go with your gut. It is so important to help children learn without shame. Put yourself in their shoes and speak to them in the way you would like to be spoken to. Sometimes when a child is giving us a tough time it is because they are having a tough time and that is the only way they can communicate that to us. Keeping this in mind can help diffuse the energy around your anger whilst still leaving you able to communicate the message and set your boundaries.

Journal Prompt

- Do you remember times as a child when an adult spoke to you in such a way that you listened and felt heard and respected?
- Do you remember times as a child when you felt shame due to the way the adult spoke to you?
- What were the differences in the different experiences?
- How would you like to be spoken to if you were a child?
- How do you want your children to feel when you are angry with them?

From my experience of being a mother, children will understand and appreciate a situation much more if you tell them you are angry, and why you are angry. Remember that it is OK to be angry, to be honest about your anger, and to own your anger around your children. You can express your anger and still be a kind, nurturing and loving mother. Being angry doesn't immediately make you mean, evil, unloving or unlovable. Modelling healthy anger can also be an excellent gift for your child, especially if you have a daughter.

Remember, your anger will escalate less if you can communicate it, and that communication does not necessarily have to be to your children. Communicate it to yourself in your journal, to your partner, mother, the delivery person or the toaster. Just communicate it.

You need to communicate your anger from a place of being assertive, vulnerable and with care and compassion. Being assertive is about giving yourself the right to have an opinion and say how you feel. In this case, 'I feel angry because of that behaviour.' It means asking for what you need, for example, 'I need you to tidy your room.' It also means disagreeing with the other person respectfully, allowing for the difference in opinion and allowing for a level of negotiation without too much compromise (another balancing act for mothers).

A case study in effective communication

The situation

Betty and her husband, Harry, have twin three-year-old daughters and don't have any family or friends who live nearby. They have different styles of communicating and expressing anger. Betty tends to suppress her anger and avoid confrontation. She finds it easier to appease and keep the peace. Betty grew up in a volatile alcoholic environment and was often scared of her mother's display of anger. She has learnt to be bland when there is conflict to not draw attention to herself. Since becoming a mother, Betty has had a fraught internal battle managing her anger so it does not spill out. Due to her painful upbringing, she has learnt to adopt the victim stance.

Harry, by contrast, grew up in a household where anger was more silent and strained. His parents were much more passive-aggressive. Harry now finds it hard to be direct with his anger. He works long shifts as a key worker for the NHS, leaving the house at 7am and arriving home at 6pm.

One tough day, Betty is feeling burnt out by the tantrums and noise of her children. They're in lockdown and it is raining so she hasn't been able to take them out. Neither child napped, so she hasn't had a break all day. At dinner-time, Betty is feeling drained and lacking in reserves. The noises from the TV and the sounds of her children shouting and playing are jarring. The smell and the heat of the cooking and the many tasks involved are stressing her out. She is desperate for Harry to come home from work.

Harry arrives just as the twins finish dinner. Betty desperately needs a break and is hoping that Harry will take over before she loses her temper, but he's in a bad mood. He looks tired and annoyed and she doesn't want to put more pressure on him. Her anger is saying, 'It is so unfair. I've been with the children all day, it's been a rubbish day, I've felt like a total failure all day. The kids have done nothing but moan and scream and shout and fight,' but she is aware that this will make Harry feel guilty and defensive. He will only withdraw, and she doesn't want that to happen.

Betty needs to express how she is feeling without Harry taking the guilt and blame on board. Harry wants to help Betty, but he is also feeling depleted and doesn't have the energy to parent.

The problem

Both parents need a break. How do Betty and Harry resolve this situation?

The communication

Harry sits on the sofa after making himself a cup of coffee. Betty waits for him to finish his coffee. She says, 'I'm feeling exhausted and overwhelmed. I can see we've both had a tough day. Can you take over for ten minutes so I can recharge, and then I'll do bath-time if you clear up? We can get a takeaway later so you don't have to cook.'

The result

Harry loves Betty and wants to help her. He takes over without feeling that Betty is trying to control him. She has a rest and then she can continue with the rest of the evening. When Harry takes over, he has a great time with the kids. He feels energised by their smiles and playfulness. Both parents' moods improve, the children feed off from this, and their behaviour gets better.

Repairing after anger

When anger has created a rupture, giving space for repair is essential. Growing up, how did people around you repair after an argument? In some households there may have been a conflict but then nothing more was said and everyone just acted as if nothing had happened. No repair made. In other households, repair is a natural part of the process of what happens after an argument. I saw an example of repair that brought tears to my eyes. It was beautifully compassionate, honouring the mother's feelings and the daughter's feelings and ultimately putting their relationship first.

I was on holiday with my sister-in-law and her children. She was having an argument with her daughter, who was upset. I heard my sister-in-law tell her daughter that she loved her, that everything was OK, not to worry and that she appreciated that her daughter had apologised for her behaviour. Then her daughter stopped crying and they carried on the day with the air cleared and both smiling and happy. My sister-in-law has a close relationship with her daughter, and I think that the relationship is so strong due to the reparative work she does with her daughter when her daughter is upset.

Compassion is a beautiful way to approach repair. Compassion is about witnessing and feeling the suffering going on in the moment and responding to that suffering. The repair can be acknowledging the suffering you and your child are experiencing. The repair can be allowing yourself to be moved and touched by that suffering. That is the most repairing and compassionate act you can do. Sometimes we respond with anger and not compassion because it is too painful to acknowledge all the pain and suffering.

To do the repair work, mothers need to first repair with themselves. I spoke to forty mothers about what helps them repair after angry outbursts, and the most significant response was time. Mothers said that they need to take time out to gain perspective. Mothers need to walk away, give themselves a timeout and an opportunity to reconnect with themselves. Maybe a 'time-in' is a better way of thinking about it – a time to go within and reconnect. Other responses were the importance of rest, and having quiet time in nature. When mothers start to feel they are getting angry too much, it is a signal that they need to rest and recharge in nature. Time to repair could look like exercising, gardening or any enjoyable thing uninterrupted. One mother I spoke to said she is learning a new language to immerse herself in an activity unrelated to her children. If the constant interruptions make you angry, sometimes being able to do something uninterrupted can be powerfully grounding and repairing. Other mums said having an action plan after rage can help repair themselves. The activities listed below helped mothers I spoke to gain perspective and heal after an anger outburst:

- Reminding myself that I am doing my best
- Talking it through with a friend
- Rationing and reflecting on the situation
- Talking it through with my partner/sister/cat/ toaster
- Letting go of the need to control my environment
- Embracing the chaos and the mess
- Acknowledging how I feel
- Breathing, yoga or meditation
- Cup of tea or glass of wine
- Throwing things
- Growling or shouting
- Singing or listening to music

Here are some words of support and wisdom for mothers, a mantra of sorts, for those struggling with their anger and need to repair. It can be useful to stick it in a place that you can read it whenever you feel the need: Be kind to yourself. Forgive yourself and forgive those around you. It is super-stressful at the moment. Take your time, take it one step at a time, one day, minute or second at a time. Parenting is hard. You are everyone's world right now, and everybody loves and appreciates you and what you are doing, even if it doesn't feel like it.

Journal Prompt

Write yourself a letter of support that you can read to yourself during tough times.

Summary

When angry, communicating from a place of vulnerability, assertiveness and care is a beautiful way to communicate your anger. It will help resolve the issue and stop you from playing out roles developed from wounds and trauma.

Repairing after anger is just as important, and can be a beautiful way to strengthen your relationship with others and yourself.

SEVEN

The Power Of Maternal Anger

A nger is a powerful emotion that can be harnessed to implement great and necessary changes. Anger respects our needs, values and identity; it keeps us and others safe from attack, abuse and disrespect. We feel anger at injustice, when we see others being hurt and treated unfairly. It was people's anger at racist violence that led to the Black Lives Matter movement and abuse against women that led to the #metoo movement. It was women being angry at the injustice of not having the vote that led to the suffragette movement. When women get together and show anger in unity, significant changes can happen.

The power of anger

Anger gives people the energy to protest and say, 'This is not right.' Anger gives you the energy to confront the threat. Anger shows that you are serious and helps you to be taken seriously. Anger can be a display of strength and power. Anger is also strongly connected with empathy. If you can connect with, and have compassion for, those suffering, you can feel anger as a response. Perhaps that is why women struggle with anger. They have been brought up to believe that women are not powerful and that anger is a male trait. Yet, women are mighty. This chapter focuses on this power and is dedicated to mothers who have used their maternal anger to campaign for significant changes and the mothers who use their anger daily to muster the strength to advocate for themselves and their families.

The value of anger

Despite the messages that have been passed down to women for centuries, feeling and expressing anger is not something we should feel guilty or ashamed of. Anger is a great asset for mothers: depending on our relationship with anger, how we respond when we are angry and how well we understand our anger, it can help keep us visible and help us to retain our identity amid the chaos of motherhood. Anger protects us. Expressing anger can be calming, which then gives us the clarity and motivation to solve problems (and we know that motherhood can bring us many).

Anger arises in painful situations, and emotional pain can be an excellent catalyst for change. Anger also drives people to be highly vigilant and sharpens our focus. Anger makes us better mothers. It makes us fight for our children and protect them. Anger gives mothers a sense of control. If we are angry and we become activated, we have told our brain we are taking control and are in charge. When I am cleaning and tidying the house in a rage, I am trying to gain control. (It is a delicate balance. Anger can also make you lose control, and we also sometimes need to accept that we don't have control.)

Anger makes you aware of injustice. Anger drives you towards your goals. Anger can stop you from playing the victim (see drama triangle), as long as you don't switch to the persecutor. Anger can increase our value through signalling to others to treat us better. Anger pushes us to reach a more profound self and to evolve as a parent. Anger covers painful feelings, and sometimes we need to bear the painful feelings underneath the anger. When we bear the painful feelings, we learn vulnerability and resilience – significant characteristics to model to our children. Feeling anger enhances emotional intelligence.[17] Anger is an excellent tool for growth and personal development. We can channel our anger to understand ourselves and our children better, especially if we adopt a stance of curiosity rather than judgement or shame.

Check in

Pause and notice your breathing. When was the last time you were really angry about something? What needed to be changed? What power and control do you have to make the changes needed?

---

17   M Ratson, 'The Value of Anger: 16 Reasons It's Good to Get Angry' (Good Therapy, 13 March 2017), www.goodtherapy.org/blog/value-of-anger-16-reasons-its-good-to-get-angry-0313175, accessed 8 September 2021

Journal Prompt

- Write a paragraph describing all the changes you would make using your anger as a motivation.

- Reflect on a time when you used your anger to keep your child safe and make a positive change in your child's life.

Needs, values and boundaries

Your needs, values and boundaries are tied up with your identity as a woman. As you become a mother, your identity and roles will shift. Mothers are often left with unmet needs, and their values may feel abandoned. In his seminal book, *Nonviolent Communication*, Rosenberg describes how unfulfilled needs are at the core of anger.[18] As my life and priorities changed when I became a mother, I felt angry that my basic needs weren't being met. When I am angry, it is useful to reflect on what needs are not being met. What values do I have to disregard?

Anger is valuable when we use it as an alarm clock to wake us up to our needs that are not being met. Applying this to motherhood, use your anger to wake yourself up to what needs are going unmet in your life. Use your anger to get to know your values, your needs and your boundaries. Often when

---

18   MB Rosenberg, *Nonviolent Communication: A language of life*, (Puddle Dancer Press, 2003)

we are angry, we turn outwards, looking for someone or something to blame for our anger. Rosenberg sees this as a violent approach and suggests that the more compassionate response is to turn inwards. I recommend reading his book for more in-depth discussion and examples of how we can express our anger in a non-violent way.

Needs

As mothers, how do we know what our needs are and consider them as essential? The word 'need' may provoke a sense of being needy within you. Sometimes, we are uncomfortable expressing our needs as we don't want to come across as needy and dependent. As soon as we have a need, we depend on an outside source to give us that need. Needs make us vulnerable. It can make us angry to have needs, and it can make us angry when we are not getting our needs met. As mothers, we have to look out for our own needs and the needs of our children. Meeting all these needs (and the needs of our partners, siblings, parents and friends) can be tiring and confusing.

Maslow was a psychologist who presented a theory that humans have a hierarchy of needs. Needs can be laid out in a pyramid shape, with basic needs at the bottom of the pyramid and more high-level needs at the top. A person needs to fulfil their basic needs before moving up the levels of the pyramid.

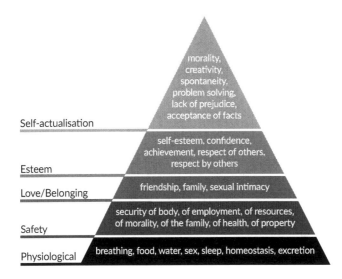

Maslow's Hierarchy of Needs. Adapted from A Maslow, 'A Theory of Human Motivation (Psychological Review, 1943)

1. **Physiological needs:** The most basic needs are physiological needs. These are the most basic human survival needs: food and water, sufficient rest, clothing and shelter, overall health and reproduction. Mothers, especially in early motherhood, are busy attending to their baby's basic needs and often do not get their most basic needs met.

2. **Safety needs:** The next level lists safety needs. Mothers need to have physical and emotional safety. As described earlier, mothers struggle to feel safe when they have experienced trauma.

A sense of safety is also skewed as mothers are hardwired to be aware of risk.

3. **Love and belonging needs:** This level is about needs relating to relationships, intimacy and a sense of belonging. As well as family and friendships, this can include social groups, sports teams and co-workers. Remember the village? If a mother hasn't got her village, her support is another fundamental need that she isn't getting. Mothers also lose a sense of belonging during maternity leave when they are no longer around co-workers and unable to attend social clubs. Friendship groups may also start to shift and change.

4. **Esteem needs:** This higher level is about self-esteem, self-respect and self-confidence. This is about how we need to believe that we are valuable and deserving of dignity. This is about confidence in our potential for personal growth. Mothers can often struggle with self-esteem if not treated with the dignity and respect deserved.

5. **Self-actualisation needs:** Self-actualisation describes the fulfilment of your full potential as a person. Sometimes called self-fulfilment needs, self-actualisation needs occupy the highest spot on Maslow's pyramid. Self-actualisation needs include education, skill development, music, athletics, design, cooking and gardening. They include caring for others and broader goals like learning a new language, travelling to new places and winning

awards. All these occupations and goals may be set aside when mothers are immersed in motherhood.[19]

It seems hard for mothers to meet all these levels of needs. Can you identify when your feelings of anger are connected to your needs not being met?

Values

Every family and home could use a strong foundation. Values can create that strong foundation. When we lose sight of our values, we can destabilise and our grounding becomes unsteady. Without values, we can lose purpose and direction. When we become mothers, our values shift. We take on new values and discard older ones. When I was in my twenties and single, the values that I had were different to the values that I have now. Sometimes, our maternal anger can be about a shift in values. Perhaps we want to cling to old values, or feel that our values are being threatened. Mothers can use their maternal anger to fight for their values.

What are your values? The questions below will help you to identify and reflect on your values:

- Think about *who* you value. Who do you admire and respect? Which mother springs to mind?

---

19   P Pichère, *Maslow's Hierarchy of Needs: Understand the true foundations of human motivation* (50Minutes.com, August 2015)

(It can be a mother from popular culture, your mother or a mother that you know.)

- When you think about this person, what characteristics does she have?

- What do you admire about her?

- What inspires you about her?

- Now think about what in life inspires you. What motivates you?

- What makes you joyful, angry, fearful or calm?

- Finally, think about when you feel your most calm and at ease. Who are you with?

- What are you doing?

Journal Prompt

Reflect on these questions and write your thoughts in your journal. This exercise will give you a greater sense of your values.

Take some time to explore the words listed below. Circle the words that resonate with you as a core list of values:

- Family
- Freedom
- Security

- Loyalty
- Intelligence
- Connection

- Creativity
- Success
- Respect
- Honesty
- Adventure
- Kindness
- Career
- Communication
- Learning
- Quality
- Courage
- Balance
- Compassion
- Fitness
- Relationship
- Knowledge
- Wellness

How do these values relate to your experience of motherhood? Which of these values do you want to foster in your children? Can you use your maternal anger to motivate you to foster what you value?

We can protect our needs and values through our boundaries. I noticed that my boundaries became fluid and vulnerable both prenatal and postnatal. Boundaries are essential as they set you apart from other people and situations. A boundary is what separates you from others. It is your protection in the same way that anger is your protection. Boundaries can stop you from becoming enmeshed and easily manipulated. Much of my anger when I was postnatal sprung from my struggle to maintain boundaries. When my values and needs felt threatened, I reacted with anger.

Strengthening boundaries means strengthening your values and taking your needs seriously. Strengthening your boundaries reflects as doing what you value. Strengthening your boundaries reflects as putting your needs first.

Having a family and spending time with family can be an essential value. Spending time alone, maintaining a hobby, maintaining self-care and wellness and spending time with friends can be of equal value. It's about balance. When we become a mother, it is easy to become out of balance. When this happens, tap into your anger and ask, 'OK, what needs rebalancing here?' Listen and take action to change.

Next time you snap at your child or lose your temper, or find yourself in a whirlwind of maternal anger and rage, if you can, stop and check in with yourself.

Check in

- How is my breathing?

- How much tension is there in my body?

- What is going on for me on an emotional level?

- What values am I losing sight of in this moment?

- Do I need to set a boundary with my child or partner? Am I overextending?

- What boundaries do I need to set?

The power of compassionate radical self-care

I want to reassure mothers grappling with maternal rage and anger (mainly if that rage has been triggered from trauma) that they can thrive as parents, especially if they can integrate trauma-informed self-care. As a mother, psychotherapist and trauma survivor, I have found that trauma-informed self-care has saved my life and sanity and made parenting a calmer and more enjoyable experience. After struggling with intense feelings of anxiety, rage and depression, I now enjoy parenting and enjoy my children.

The impact of maternal rage and anger, especially if coming from a place of trauma, can be profound. There are many ways to manage, heal and resolve feelings of rage and trauma, but it is tough to access support and services when you are in the early throes of parenthood. Trauma-informed self-care is essential in surviving parenting. Self-care, literally meaning 'taking care of oneself and putting your needs first; looking after yourself as you would your child', is essential to healing and thriving when traumatised. The self-care needs to be trauma-informed or you are at risk of re-traumatisation.

A trauma-informed self-care practice understands and considers the pervasive nature of trauma and promotes healing and recovery. Trauma-informed self-care is essential to thriving while parenting, especially as many parents will be parenting while carrying trauma. Self-care needs to be more than paying lip service, or we risk frustrating overwhelmed parents at best, and re-traumatising them at worst.

Parents face many daily challenges and often find that their needs come last and are even forgotten. Self-care is about pausing, taking a breath and checking in with our needs at that moment. Is there an unmet need here? If so, how can I make this need a priority? As a parent with young children, I appreciate you feeling exhausted and that there is little time or space for yourself and your needs. I am sure you appreciate and know that self-care will help you through the chaos, the tantrums and the sleep deprivation but even the mention of self-care will seem frustrating when you have barely had time to shower or eat properly.

Self-care is essential if we are to survive and thrive in the early days, weeks, months and years of parenting. Radical self-care is the idea that you have a *responsibility* to take care of *yourself* before taking care of *others*. Radical self-care practices focus on our moment-to-moment needs and our attempt to meet those needs. It focuses on nurturing our inner child while we are nurturing our children.

Society and social media can make us feel like bad parents simply because we want to put ourselves first and have some 'me time' away from the children.

Wanting time to yourself and space to take care of yourself does not make you a bad mother. It doesn't make you anything: it just is. I get annoyed when I hear the phrase, 'you can't give from an empty cup, so refill it first'. This gives the impression that self-care is still for the benefit of others.

Self-care is an individual need for the sake of the individual only. This should not be seen as radical.

Please make yourself a priority. It will make a difference. Why shouldn't you take care of yourself? Be honest here. Are you taking care of yourself as much as you could? Is there more room and space for self-care in your day? Could you make it more of a priority? The challenge to writing about self-care and motherhood is that there are some fundamental barriers to accessing self-care. There is no point in telling you to make a list of self-care practices when you don't have the time, energy or resources to put them into place. It only feels frustrating to feel that you need to be doing more when you feel you are already doing so much.

We must take care of ourselves in the early stages of motherhood and put our needs first, especially as there are many competing needs to prioritise. Often, we may confuse our wants and needs. Hopefully the previous chapters have helped you to create enough space around your anger and internal process to understand your needs and what is lacking.

Check in

- Do I need a drink or am I hungry?

- Do I need the toilet?

- Am I in pain or feeling unwell?

- Am I feeling lonely and disconnected today?

- Do I need a hug?

- Has someone annoyed me today?

- What did I consume yesterday? Could my diet or alcohol intake be impacting my mood? What does my body need instead?

- Do I need to let go and enjoy some comfort food, or do I need to eat more healthy food?

- Do I need to relax because I am feeling too wired? Can I give my brain some downtime with Netflix or a meditation?

- Does my mind need stimulation? Can I listen to an audiobook in the car or with my headphones?

When you check in with yourself regularly, you will start to give yourself the things you need naturally. If this seems overwhelming, especially for new mothers in the early stages, pick one self-care practice and try and stick to that. Pick one you genuinely enjoy, or you won't keep it up. Keep it up, and you won't burn out – and why *should* you burn out?

I needed to make sure that by midday each day, I had ten minutes to myself to drink coffee in the garden. I also needed to make sure that I had showered before I got the children ready. These two things made such a difference to how I felt throughout the day. A friend of mine always made sure she had an hour to go for a run each day at 5pm. She would use that time to listen to music or podcasts or even speak to a friend on the phone. A simple act of self-care can even be just spending a minute each day checking in with yourself or doing a three-minute body scan. The Calm app has some effective but quick meditations.

For survivors of trauma, it's essential to be aware of how much we are taking care of ourselves and prioritising our needs as survivors often struggle to prioritise needs. When I have gone into compliant mode, I recognise that I am stressed and depleted. It's a familiar position that I learnt as a child. Compliant mode means I have gone into survival mode. I am simply surviving and not thriving. To thrive, I need to reassert my boundaries, reach out for help, and check in with friends. To move from survival mode to thriving as quickly as possible, you need to have a healthy sense of humour and perspective, and check in with someone you trust. Start saying no and asserting your needs, and then you will naturally start prioritising self-care. The following story is to show how prioritising self-care was a turning point in my personal experience as a mother.

Jo's story

I would experience a lot of intense anxiety over leaving the house, with or without the children. If I left the house with the children, I would get intrusive thoughts of bad things happening to them. What if I mistimed crossing the road and we all got hit by a car? Before even leaving the house, I would feel stuck with indecision. What if I chose the wrong destination? Would it be better if I went somewhere else? What if I couldn't cope or manage? This fearfulness was exhausting and made me bad-tempered. I was struggling with gaining perspective. I was struggling with trusting myself and my judgement and abilities as a parent.

As soon as I started prioritising self-care, I started to feel more confident and trusting in myself. I felt more grounded and clearer to problem-solve and was able to be in the moment. Self-care brings you back into your window of tolerance and can be so empowering. To get to the point where I could start prioritising self-care, I needed to spend time giving myself the self-compassion that was really needed.

Self-care should not be another thing that mothers feel adds to the mental load. It isn't another stick to beat yourself up. Simply pausing in your day to acknowledge your own needs or gently saying no to something and holding a boundary is self-care. Not doing the washing up and watching *Finding Nemo* with your child is self-care. Jumping in the warm bubble-bath with your baby is self-care. Ordering a takeaway is self-care. Going for a walk with your baby is self-care. Visiting a farm with your toddler is self-care. Doing an internal meditation while breastfeeding is self-care, and so is watching Netflix. Anything that refuels you and nurtures you when you need nurturing is self-care.

Realistic self-care practices

Busy mothers doing their best should be able to find some time for the following self-care practices which integrate Maslow's hierarchy of needs.

1. Each day, make sure you are never too hungry, thirsty, cold, hot or tired. Rest when given an opportunity.

2. Self-soothing, tapping, meditation and yoga poses will give you a sense of safety throughout the day. The more you practise, the less time it will take out of your day.

3. Spend some time each week doing something outside the experience of motherhood, even if it is something as simple as doing a puzzle, watching a film or reading a book. If you don't have time in your week for even an hour, you need to look at how you can bring that into your life.

4. Write, draw, sing, paint, dance, bake, go to the farm or go for a swim. You can do all these things with your children (or not).

Journal Prompt

Keep a journal of your radical self-care practices and the difference it makes to your day. If you are in the early stages of motherhood, write a few words down or send them as a message to yourself. If you have more time, explore and reflect in more depth.

Summary

The power of maternal anger can motivate women to protect themselves and protect others. Anger can mobilise mothers to stand up for what they value and ask for and get what they need. Anger can move mothers to discover the power of self-care. Keep discovering what your anger can do for you and use it as a force for good and a force for change. Take care of yourself and keep putting yourself first. Discover your unmet needs and make it a priority to fulfil them, as this will undoubtedly reduce your anger and create less harm for yourself and others.

Conclusion

When mothers are angry, they are navigating complex emotions that, if left unchecked and unreflected upon, can lead to toxic behaviours and words and ruptures in relationships. The good news is that anger can take many forms and has many uses. What mothers need is the space for reflection and the invitation to appreciate the context surrounding anger. Mothers need the tools to ground and find a place of stability and strength when anger manifests. Mothers also need the reassurance that there is always the opportunity to repair, and the confidence and sense of entitlement to develop self-care practices.

The purpose of this book was to give all that to mothers who are struggling. To empower mothers to work through their process so they don't harm their children. The aim has not been to calm down a mother's anger and dismiss or minimise it, but to show mothers that their anger is valuable and essential in understanding themselves, their children and their situation.

I have learnt so much about anger through being a woman, and especially a mother living through a pandemic. The process of becoming a mother to my two beautiful children has given me the confidence in allowing myself to be angry and expressing that anger in a confident and assertive, yet safe, way. I have strengthened my relationships with myself, my husband and my children. Through writing this book and speaking to mothers about maternal anger, I have learnt so much. I have felt calmer and less angry, having written this out and reflected and thought about my anger. This calmness has given me the clarity of thought and confidence to be angry, and angry in a constructive way. I hope this book is a constructive expression of my anger.

There is so much wisdom inside each mother grappling with their anger. The strength and determination to be better mothers, to be better women, and live their lives with integrity despite real feelings of rage. Each mother I spoke to has so much to give to the world, and I hope I have given the complex experience of maternal anger the justice it deserves. I also hope I have made you, the reader, a little less rageful and a little more empowered. I hope you have felt heard.

I hope that reading this book has been as cathartic for you as it has been for me to write. I wrote this book during the Covid-19 pandemic. I believe the lockdowns, social distancing, and the ever-shifting restrictions made me confront my anger more intensely than if I had been able to distract or soothe myself with my usual self-care and other activities. Sometimes we can use self-care and support from others to avoid or distract from the complex feelings of anger that can emerge when we are mothers. Sometimes we can use it to give us the resilience to withstand our anger.

With two small children, it was tough to not be angry during the pandemic. I hope that this book has given you space to develop a new relationship with your anger. One where you are in control, you aren't afraid of your feelings, and you are aware of the power and responsibility around expressing anger around children. I hope I have given the topic of maternal anger justice.

If you are struggling with maternal anger and rage, the next step in your journey is to reach out to a therapist, create a support network, keep journaling and keep up your self-care practice. Writing this book was an act of self-care, and I hope that it has inspired you in some way. Please, approach motherhood with tremendous respect and always speak to yourself and your children with compassion and love. The world needs more compassion and less hostility. I hope reading this book has been an act of self-care for you. Thank you for giving me your time to read.

Parenting is hard work but women are mighty! You got this, Mamma!

Resources

Books

N Stadlen, *What Mothers Do: especially when it looks like nothing* (Hachette Digital, 2004)

M Scotland, *Birth Shock: How to recover from birth trauma – why 'at least you've got a healthy baby' isn't enough* (Pinter & Martin Ltd., First ed, September 2020)

A Mathur, *Mind Over Mother: Every mum's guide to worry and anxiety in the first years* (Piatkus, May 2020)

M Scotland, *Why Postnatal Depression Matters* (Pinter & Martin, 2015)

J Brant, *Parenting with PTSD: the impact of childhood abuse on parenting* (CreateSpace Independent Publishing Platform, October 2017)

H Lerner, *The Dance of Anger: A woman's guide to changing the pattern of intimate relationships* (Element Books, January 2004)

Useful websites

Naomi Stadlen, author and psychotherapist: https://naomistadlen.com

Pink Therapy: www.pinktherapy.com

Hand in Hand Parenting: www.handinhandparenting.org

Miranda Fairhall, psychotherapist and coach: https://attuneforconnection.com

MIND: www.mind.org.uk

The EMDR Association: https://emdrassociation.org.uk

Acknowledgements

My husband who has taught me so much about my anger. Who learnt quickly that sometimes crying means I am angry, and sometimes when I am angry means I am sad. I couldn't have written this and survived the early years of motherhood without your big heart and belief in me.

Thank you to my mum. I love you.

My sister, for our late-night chats and having my back.

Julie, for your generous spirit.

My sisters-in-law, who model motherhood with such love and compassion.

My wonderful friends; thank you for all your kindness and support, the WhatsApp chats, the late night swims and sharing of stories.

A massive thank you to all of the mothers I interviewed and spoke to along the way.

The Illustrator

Laura Vahabzadeh is an art psychotherapist who works both in a young offender institution and a secondary school. Through her work she has seen how powerful visual imagery can be used to express emotions and experiences that people are unable to do through words.

She felt honoured to create work based on her own experiences, and those of other women, to help support people's understanding of this text through a visual medium. Laura feels that people find art a more acceptable way to express feelings or experiences that are often viewed as unspeakable or taboo in society. She has used her own art to help process her feelings – especially those of anger and frustration over the challenges of being a single parent.

Whilst discussing experiences with other women, she realized that many people struggle to express their feelings on this topic or feel it is unacceptable to feel these feelings. However, as a mother and artist she was able to explore the full range of emotions which surround motherhood by being open and honest through her art making; this helped open up these conversations and allow women a safe space to explore and express their own emotions.

The Author

 Cristalle Hayes is an exis-
tential and trauma-informed
UKCP registered psychotherapist who runs a private practice from her home in North
London. Cristalle is also a
qualified EMDR practitioner.
Cristalle has shared therapeu-
tic spaces with many women and mothers struggling to
navigate their anger and their place in the world. After
studying religious studies and philosophy at university,
Cristalle went on to work in secondary schools teaching
world religions and ethics. When Cristalle isn't working with clients or writing, she is busy being a mum to
two young boys, always with a coffee on the go and

sneaking away for long swims and to read from her ever-growing pile of books.

Please reach out to me if you have any questions or comments.

⊕ www.cristallehayestherapy.com

Made in the USA
Columbia, SC
04 May 2023